We would like to take a minute to thank the below listed contributors to Secrets. Without their assistance this book would not have been possible.

Secrets Contributors:

Editor: ArticleEditor, www.fiverr.com/articleditor

Reviewers: Monique Jones, Sylvia Wilson, Destiny Berry and Avis Dillard

Cover design: Mad House Design Inc, madhousedesigninc@gmail.com

Public Relations: Virginia Wiggins

I0134751

Prologue

My name is Kyanna Black, the youngest daughter of John and Rhonda Black. My parents, brothers, Markus and Damien, all lived in Belmont Heights until tragedy struck us. I was just a young girl back then, but I want to tell my brother's story.

Markus' childhood sucked. Our father, John Black, was an alcoholic who abused us. My mother got it the worse, but we all suffered. Markus could never understand why Momma stayed with Daddy for so long.

Markus was the oldest, and he always tried to look out for Damien and me, at least as much as he could. It caused him a lot of pain, but he always felt it was worth it to protect us. In fact, I counted on it.

Momma was the greatest. She did everything she could to protect us from our abusive father. The only thing she didn't do was leave him. When Markus asked her why she stayed, she would always tell him that her children needed a father and a mother. Markus didn't think we needed our father at all. It wasn't until later that I realized that Markus was right, we didn't need him.

Secrets (Silent Screams in the Dark)

Righteous Productions – November 2016
PO Box 383
White Plains MD 20695
admin@righteouspro.com
www.righteouspro.com
Facebook: www.facebook.com/righteouspro
Twitter: @righteousprofl
Instagram: @righteousproductions

Gerald C. Anderson, Sr.
ganderson@geraldcandersonsr.com
www.geraldcandersonsr.com
Facebook: www.facebook.com/geraldcandersonsr
Twitter: @geraldcanderson
Instagram: @geraldcandersonsr

1

The school bus pulled up to 22nd Street and dropped off the kids who attended Chamberlain Senior High School. Markus saw Renata, who had already gotten off the bus, standing outside waiting for her friends. He thought she was the most beautiful girl ever. He hoped no one saw him staring at her, but he couldn't help himself. She was breathtaking.

He wanted so bad to be her boyfriend that he often asked himself, 'Why would she like me?' He rationalized that she wouldn't like him because he didn't play sports. It didn't help that his dad always told him that he wasn't worth anything. He found himself looking so hard at Renata; he almost didn't hear Andra, "You getting off?"

She startled him, "Oh yeah, I guess I was daydreaming or something." Andra smiled, "Yeah I bet you were."

Andra was a good friend. Markus figured she knew about his crush but didn't say anything. He often wondered if she told Renata. "Hi, Markus," he was startled again. It was Renata. He didn't know what he was going to say. He wanted to say something but what? "Um...hey...um, hi...Renata." He felt stupid. Nothing ever came out right.

Renata smiled and walked away. He thought, "*I blew it. My dad was right. I'm not worth anything.*"

***

Markus was coming down the sidewalk to their apartment. The neighbors were gathered outside, and he could hear his dad yelling. Markus dropped his books and ran to their apartment. Miss Susie Mae tried to stop him from going in, but she couldn't. He jerked away from her and dashed inside.

Markus swung the door open, and there was his father, standing over his mother like he was some sort of god. He wasn't... he was evil and mean. Markus hated him. He dove at his father, but his father grabbed Markus and threw him to the side like a ragdoll.

Rhonda shouted, "No, don't hurt my baby!" John shouted back, "Shut up!"

John slapped Rhonda, and she fell backward to the chair. Markus heard his sister, Kyanna, crying upstairs and commotion coming from outside. He tried to get up, but his father kicked him back down, "Oh, you think you're a man now? Let's see what you got, you good for nothing little punk!"

Markus was relieved when he heard sirens coming from the street. This was the one time his father wouldn't get to teach him a lesson. His father ran out the back door and Markus helped his mother.

Markus held her as she was crying. He begged, "Mom, please let's leave. Please, Momma, let's just go and never come back."

Damien was Markus's little brother. He and Kyanna joined Markus and their mother. If nothing else, there was a strong bond of love between the four of them, but Markus worried about Damien.

***

The police finally left, but Markus knew something they didn't. His mom would eventually let his dad return. His dad would always hide away somewhere, probably with his girlfriend, and then come back. For a few days, they would have peace and harmony in the house.

Damien was looking at Markus, "Why you staring at me like that?" Damien shrugged his shoulders, "I don't know."

"Yes you do, what's up?"

Damien asked, "Why doesn't Mom just do like Dad says, so he won't have to beat her like that?"

"What? Mom doesn't deserve that. Why are you saying that?! Dad is a punk and a coward. He wouldn't beat a man like that."

Kyanna hit Markus in the arm, "Daddy just needs help."

Markus was angry at both of them. His mother's forgiving nature was being passed on to Kyanna. Meanwhile, Damien believed their father was in the right for treating their mother like property. He could only hope that they weren't headed for the same life that his mom and dad were living.

He looked Kyanna square in the eyes, "Kyanna, Dad isn't going to get help. He thinks that's the way you show love. He doesn't love us."

She started to cry, "Yes, he does!" She ran out the kitchen and upstairs crying. He couldn't get through to her now. She believed her father loved her no matter what. She refused to accept what she saw going on in their home.

Damien looked down at his hamburger and fries, "She's stupid. Mommy is the one who needs help."

Markus felt the impulse to slap Damien, but he held it back. After all, he would then be no better than his father. How could Damien say that about their mother? How could anyone condone abuse? Markus thought, "*Daddy often beats her for no reason. He beats us for no reason. How could Damien see Momma as wrong?*"

"Don't say that, Momma is innocent! Daddy is the one that needs help."

"Yeah, whatever." Damien threw his food in the trash and left the kitchen. Markus was alone when his mother came in the room. She sat down next to him and put her hand on his arm, "I know you don't agree with my choosing to stay here with your dad, but someday you will see. I can't leave right now. You, your brother and sister are too young, and I can't do it all by myself. The money he brings in supports us."

"Mom, I would rather eat out of the trash can than suffer this life."

She smiled. Rhonda's smile could always light up the room. Markus didn't agree with her, but he had to trust her because she was all he had.

She said, "You are not worthless. You are a very intelligent and wonderful young man. Don't ever let your father's words destroy your confidence. I know you better than him
, and you are a great young man."

"Mom, how do you tell a girl you like her?"

Rhonda smiled hard. Markus' question must have ignited something in her soul.

"You just come out and tell her how you feel. A girl wants to know the truth more than anything else. Don't play with her emotions and by no means don't you lie to her."

"What if she rejects me?"

"Then you find someone else to fall in love with. Rejection is a part of life, and sometimes you'll find that right person and sometimes you won't. One thing is for sure, you always regret never asking."

Markus nodded. She was making good sense. Renata wouldn't know how he felt if he didn't tell her, but he was so afraid of rejection that he became clumsy around her. He could never get the words out right.

"Mom, every time I'm around her I get so nervous that I can't tell her how I feel."

She squeezed his arm, "Son, that's natural. Just practice in the mirror a few times. Imagine it in your mind and then go up to her and tell her how you feel. I'm sure she will appreciate it. Once she answers, then you go from there. I have confidence in you, Markus."

She stood up and walked out the room. Damien and Kyanna could be heard fighting over the television upstairs.

Markus was deep in thought about Renata. She was so beautiful, but he felt he was so ugly. *"Why would she want me?"* he asked himself. *"Why would anyone want anything to do with the abused kid of the neighborhood?"*

Markus then thought about what people were going to say tomorrow at school. He imagined some of the names they would call him and prepared for the onslaught. He knew Renata, Andra and Paula Blocker, his neighbor, and closest female friend wouldn't pick on him, but the others would. He wanted to stand up to them, but fighting just wasn't in his nature, especially after seeing all the pain inflicted by his father. He didn't want anything to do with fighting.

The phone interrupted his thoughts, and he went to answer it, "Hello."

"Hey Markus, you okay?" It was Paula. She was always checking on him. She had been his friend since kindergarten. Markus answered, "Yeah, I'm okay. He's gone, so we should have some peace for a few days."

"Good, I hope he stays away. He's so mean."

Markus chuckled, "You telling me! I don't want to go to school because everyone will laugh at me."

"What? No one is laughing at you. Why you think that?"

"Because I'm weak and ugly."

"Oh my God, Markus. No, you're not. You're handsome and the best guy I know."

"Thanks, Paula. You've always been my friend, and I appreciate you and Diane."

Markus heard Paula's mom call her in the background. Paula said, "I have to go, but you better be at school tomorrow. Don't make me come get you."

Markus laughed, "Okay, I'll be there. Bye, Paula."

"Bye, Markus."

Rhonda dragged Damien back in the room, "Damien Black, where did you get that from?"

"Dad, he said don't let a woman tell you what to do! Kyanna tried to tell me what she was going to watch on TV, so I put her in her place like Dad does you."

Kyanna was crying upstairs, and Rhonda broke out in tears. Markus was frozen in place. Again he wanted to slap Damien, but instead he was angry because Damien learned his behavior from their father.

2

It was lunchtime at school and the morning was pretty uneventful. Markus didn't get to sit near Renata on the bus ride, but there she was two tables away from him with her friends. He couldn't believe it had been two years since he fell for her and still he hadn't said anything to her about it. He felt like his father was right, he was truly a wimp.

To Markus, she was the prettiest girl in the group. If she would only be alone, then he would muster up the courage to go talk to her. *"Well, if only,"* he thought.

Cleveland startled him, "What's up Markus?" "Hey man, nothing I'm just sitting here eating lunch. What's up with you?"

"Man, your Dad is a trip. I saw him running up on Lake. He must have been at it again huh?" Markus was still looking at Renata and daydreaming when Cleveland pushed him on his shoulder, "Bruh..."

"Oh…yeah man, he on the run again but it doesn't matter my mom will just let him back in again."

"Why do that?"

"Who knows, I just want to get out of here."

Cleveland smiled, "That ain't all you want. Which one you want to hit?"

Markus was shocked, "Hit? I'm not that kind of guy man."

"Bro if anyone knows that, I know that. It's just a term we use that's all. So which one…no, let me guess…hmmmm, Andra? No, wait…Veda, yeah I bet it's Veda."

Markus smiled, "Nope, neither of them." He stood up, "Well I have to get to algebra. We have a big test today, and I'm not even prepared."

Cleveland laughed sarcastically, "You…not prepared…come on man, really?"

Markus snickered, glanced once more at Renata and walked away. He imagined a life where he wasn't being abused, and he was brave enough to tell Renata that he loved her.

***

Markus was sitting on the bus praying this would be the day Renata would sit next to him. It didn't happen. Instead, she sat by her best friend, Andra and they laughed and talked.

Markus just sat in deep thought by himself. He had two more years to live at home and wanted to get out of there. But he couldn't leave his mother and siblings behind. He needed to find a way to get all of them out. He was worried about his little brother. Instead of hating his father like he did, Damien was becoming his father.

The bus pulled out of the school yard and headed to Belmont Heights. Paula broke Markus's silence, "Hey Markus, how was your day?"

"It was cool. I had no issues. Yours?"

"Nothing special. Didn't I tell you no one would pick on you?"

Markus smiled, "Yeah you did." Diane was sitting in the seat across the aisle from them. Diane asked, "How do you think you did on that algebra test Markus?"

"I don't know, I think I got at least a "B". How do you think you did?"

Diane laughed, "Probably a "C", maybe a "B" if I got that last one right. It was tough."

"Yeah, Mr. Jackson is a hard teacher."

Cleveland chimed in from the seat behind them, "Yeah, but you should see his daughter! She's in the seventh grade, but Jasmine is so fine."

Paula and Shelia laughed. Paula said, "You better leave that young girl alone."

Cleveland replied, "She may be young, but she got it going on. I can't imagine what she's going to look like when she's older." Paula said, "They gonna lock you up."

Cleveland said, "You ask any dude on this bus about Jasmine and see what they say."

He threw his hands up and sat back in his seat.

Markus was amazed at how easily Cleveland could relay his feelings about girls. He couldn't say one thing about how he felt about Renata, but Cleveland didn't hold anything back.

Cleveland's family was much better than Markus'. His father took time to teach him everything. Markus would go to their house and wouldn't leave because it was so peaceful. Cleveland told him they had their issues, but it wasn't anything like Markus's house.

The bus pulled up to the 22nd Street stop, and everyone got off. Markus dreaded this moment. He had to go home. At least at school, it was peaceful. No one yelled at him, and most of the kids didn't know his home situation. Paula was right the kids didn't make fun of him, but he could tell in most of their eyes that they felt sorry for him.

That didn't help either. Being pitied by everyone wasn't something he liked much. Someday he hoped to be idolized by millions but then the words of his father took over and he felt he would be lucky to live to see 18.

As Markus got closer to his house, he got nervous. He asked, "*I wonder did she let him back in already? God, I hope not!*"

Damien came running out of the house. Markus asked, "Where you going?"

"To see my girl, if it's any business of yours."

Markus waited before going in the house. He saw another girl that he knew was having abuse problems. He thought they would get together because they both shared the same issue.

LaJuan Craig waved at Markus and smiled. He waved back. She was only in the ninth grade, but she was pretty. Markus noticed how she covered her bruises all the time. He wanted to talk to her but felt she was just like him and didn't want to talk to anyone.

He finally decided to go inside. It was quiet. Kyanna was watching TV downstairs, and he heard his mom moving around upstairs. He didn't hear his father's voice at all. He asked Kyanna, "Did he come back?"

Kyanna frowned, "No."

"Why you frowning?"

Kyanna responded, "Because I miss Daddy. He always helps me with my homework."

Markus sat his books down, "I can help you Kyanna."

"Daddy said you're stupid and not to listen to you."

Markus's head dropped. That hurt him that his baby sister was being taught to hate him, but then she brighten his day.

"But I don't believe that. You're my big brother, and I think you're the smartest person I know."

Markus smiled, "Thanks, Kyanna. You had me going there for a minute."

She smiled back, "Can you help me with my math?"

"Sure. Let's see what we got."

***

Markus was finished helping his little sister with her homework and relaxing on his bed. As he usually did, he imagined a better life for all of them. He wondered what life would be like married to Renata, what their kids would be like and maybe a job making more money than he could imagine. He thought, *"That would be my American dream!"*

From out of nowhere, he heard screaming outside. He looked out the window and saw LaJuan running down the sidewalk. Her father was right behind her and closing fast.

Markus shouted, "Leave her alone!" The man stopped and looked up at the window. Markus knew he saw him, but he didn't care. Her father rolled his eyes and went back home.

Markus couldn't see LaJuan anymore. He ran downstairs, and his mom and sister were standing outside the back door.

Rhonda said to her son, "You shouldn't have butted in. That's their business and not ours, you understand."

Markus rolled his eyes at her, "No I don't." He walked in the house and wondered why everyone considered abuse to be a family secret. He vowed when he grew up he was going to do what he could to stop abuse.

Damien came in from the front door, "Did you see what happened to LaJuan? Yeah her dad whipped that behind!"

"Why do you think that's funny? It's not funny at all especially since the same thing happens to us! Abuse isn't funny, and someone needs to come in this neighborhood and clean house."

Damien replied, "You're just a punk like dad said. He's toughening us up for the real world, and you just can't handle it. I'm a man, and I can handle. No woman is going to make me look bad."

Damien turned and walked away. Markus couldn't understand how Damien had come to think the way his father does.

They both live in the same house, yet they are worlds apart on the abuse issue. Rhonda and Kyanna came back in the house. Kyanna looked sad as she walked by Markus.

Rhonda said to her, "Kyanna go take your bath, honey."

Kyanna hugged her big brother then ran upstairs.

Markus asked, "What's wrong with her mom?"

Rhonda answered, "She's a little upset at what happened just now."

Markus angrily responded, "She should be. When is this going to stop? One day it's us and the next it's our neighbors. Somebody has got to do something. We've got to stop living in secret!"

"Don't raise your voice to me boy. I'm still your mother whether you agree with my decisions or not. Now we can't barge into everyone else's business, and I surely don't want them in ours. Our family isn't the best, but it's not the worst either."

Markus nodded, "That's your logic? I hate it here mom!" Markus angrily walked away upstairs to check on his baby sister. His mother didn't move.

***

It was an hour later, and Markus was finishing the dishes. He looked out the kitchen window and could see LaJuan sitting by the tree. She looked like she was crying. He decided to go against his mother's wishes and see what he could do to help.

He went outside and walked over to LaJuan. She was holding her blouse closed. Apparently, the buttons had been ripped off. Markus asked, "Are you okay?"

She rolled her eyes at him. He kneeled down and said, "Sorry that was a stupid question. Do you want to talk?"

LaJuan said, "You go through it too don't you?"

Markus sat down, "Yeah. My dad hates me, and I hate him. I can't understand why my mom won't leave him."

LaJuan wiped away a tear, "Why don't you just leave? You're 16. If I was that old, I'd run away. At least the police wouldn't bring you back."

"You ran away?"

LaJuan held up three fingers, "Three times and each time they brought me back. My mom covered for him each time."

"Wow...I've thought about running away, but I couldn't do it because my brother and sister are still here. I couldn't leave them behind."

LaJuan smiled, "Your sister is sweet. Your brother is a bastard."

Markus was shocked, "Why you say that?"

"You don't know how he is at school. He's becoming just like your dad."

Markus knew it already, but he didn't want to accept it. He switched the subject, "What did your dad do to you?"

"He's not my real dad. My mom remarried two years ago. My real father died five years ago."

Markus said, "I'm sorry. Why does she let him abuse you?"

"Same as your mom. They don't want to leave because they think they won't be able to survive without them. My stepdad controls all the money. He gives my mom a freaking allowance. All the time he has his way with me whenever he can."

Markus was shocked, "What do you mean?"

LaJuan's mother grabbed her by the arm, "LaJuan get in this house now. You know you need to stop lying to this boy."

LaJuan looked at Markus with pleading eyes, "See what I mean."

LaJuan's mother dragged her in the house. She was only 14, and her mother was more than twice her size. She could never fight her off. Markus felt deeply sick for her inside. When he turned to walk back in the house, he heard a scream from LaJuan's house. He started to cry.

3

It was a hot Saturday morning in Florida and Damien was walking back from the store. His mom sent them to get some breakfast items. He was embarrassed because he didn't have enough money and had to put some items back.

Damien was startled when his dad stepped from behind a tree. Damien ran to John Black and hugged him.

John asked, "Where you coming from?"

Damien answered, "The store. Mom sent me to get some things to make breakfast for us, but she didn't give me enough money. I had to put some things back. It was so embarrassing."

John said, "Come on, let's go back and get the other stuff."

"Are you coming home, Dad?"

John sighed, "Maybe if your mom doesn't call the police like our nosy neighbors did."

Damien said angrily, "They need to stay out of our family's business!"

John smiled, "See you understand boy." He knelt down and looked Damien in the eyes, "You, you're going to be special. You understand how to deal with things the way I do. You can't let no woman push you around. The minute they do they own you and you don't want that. You get it?"

"Yeah Dad, I get it. I just wish Markus understood."

John stood up, and they walked to the store. He had his arm around Damien, "That boy is worthless, Damien. Don't be a nerd like him. I see you got music in your blood like your old man. Me and you, we're a lot alike. That brother of yours will never amount to anything."

"Dad, when I grow up I'm going to get into the music business. I'm going to be the guy who finds the talent and signs them to a deal. That way I get paid in multiple ways!"

John hugged him tightly and smiled, "See, you've been paying attention son."

John and Damien arrived back at the
apartment and came in the back door.
Rhonda froze when she saw John.
Damien excitedly said, "Mom, look who I
ran into? Dad wants to come back!"

Rhonda said, "Damien, go in the living
room with your brother and sister."

"Why?"

Rhonda sternly said, "Go, boy!"

Damien left the room, but he could see his
parents talking. He was angry with his
mom. He said to himself, *"Why does she
have to be so stupid. Let him back!"*

Damien positioned himself so he could
hear the conversation.

John said, "Honey, you know I love you,
and I promise I won't do it again. We can
make this work."

Rhonda eased away, "You say that every
time John. How can I keep believing you?
How can you ask me to? What about the

kids? You got Damien thinking this is the way you are supposed to treat women. It sickens me to see how he acts sometimes."

John eased over to her and put his hands on her shoulders. He attempted to kiss her, but she turned her head. He put his fingers on her chin and turned it slowly back to him then he kissed her on the lips.

Damien smiled. He knew his dad was back again and it would feel like home again. He clenched his fist, "Yeah."

Markus stared coldly at him. They would never see eye to eye and Damien knew it.

Damien stared coldly back at his brother, "What you looking at...punk?" He walked upstairs, happy that his parents were back together again.

***

It was later in the evening when Damien was hanging out with his girlfriend, Brittani. The two of them were sitting on Brittani's porch talking.

Damien said, "I'm so happy my dad is home."

Brittani moved her head from his shoulder, "What? As mean as he treats your mom, you're glad?"

Damien frowned, "Everyone talks about my dad so bad. I would appreciate it if my girl would support me. I'm the one living there you aren't."

Brittani replied, "You're right. You know better than I do but everyone talks about it. My mom thinks I don't hear, but I do hear her talking to her friends sometimes. She doesn't like me talking to you either."

Damien put his arm around her, "But what about you baby? You wanna talk to me?"

Brittani smiled and gently pushed him back, "Yeah, you know I do. Now stop before my mom catches you and runs you away."

Damien smiled and leaned back, "Okay. One day baby I'm going to be the biggest artist and repertoire man on the planet. I'll get all the talent lined up and working for me. I'll have so much money I won't be able to spend it all."

Brittani laughed, "You gonna spend it on me?"

"You know it, baby! I'll buy you a big house and the best car around."

"A Benz?"

Damien kissed her lightly on the lips, "If that's what my baby wants, then that's what she'll get."

"Brittani!" Brittani cringed as her mom called her name, "Oh my gosh, already." Damien nodded his head. Brittani answered, "Yes ma'am."

"Come in the house, you know it's getting late."

Brittani sarcastically laughed and said under her breath, "Really...it's only seven?"

Damien said, "Your mom is too strict."

"Does that mean you're going to break up with me, Mr. Damien Black?"

Damien kissed her and tried to put his hand between her legs. Brittani closed her legs. They both jumped when her mom shouted, "If you want that hand you better move it now!"

Damien jumped up and ran, "Bye Brittani!"

He never heard her answer, and he was running pass the row of apartments in Belmont Heights to get back to his own.

***

By the time he got home Damien was completely out of breath. He looked over and saw LaJuan. He didn't like her, and she didn't care for him either. They were rivals at school and home. One day Damien wanted to fight her because he grabbed her breast and she slapped him.

The only thing that stopped Damien was one of the teachers in school. He swore he would get his revenge one day, but he was too tired from running to even curse at her like he would usually do.

He just frowned at her, and she returned the gesture and shot him a bird. Damien walked into the house and saw his mom sitting on his dad's lap. That made him happy. His dad had successfully returned home. He knew his big brother would hate that and he took pleasure in knowing that.

Rhonda asked, "You hungry Damien?"

Damien answered, "Yeah a little."

Rhonda replied, "Let me fix your plate."

John interrupted, "Let him fix his own plate. You stay right here. He's 14years old he can handle it. Ain't that right son?"

"Yeah Dad, I got it." Damien high-fived his Dad. They had a good relationship. Damien admired his dad and wanted to be just like him.

Markus came in the back door and stared at Damien. Damien was singing and making a plate of food. He didn't pay his big brother any attention. Markus went into the living and Damien heard his mom, "Hey baby, where you been?"

Markus answered, "At the park playing basketball."

Damien snickered, "Really, that's a joke."

Rhonda said, "Go upstairs and get washed up sweetheart so you can make yourself a plate."

John snapped, "Stop treating him like a baby. He's freaking 16, be a man, boy!"

Rhonda said, "Don't yell at him."

Damien came in the room, "Want a beer, Dad?" Damien knew a part of him didn't want his dad to hit his mom again. They had just got back together. He wanted this moment to last a while longer. His dad was rolling his eyes at him like he was thinking he was a punk like Markus. Damien was afraid he would get beat now.

John turned his head away from Damien, "Yeah bring me a cold one, son."

Damien was relieved. His dad called him "son" so that meant he didn't think he was a punk. He never called Markus "son" because he didn't respect him. His dad thought Markus was soft and weak. He didn't care for people who were smart. Damien felt he could never be smart like his older brother so he decided to be tough like his dad.

***

After Damien finished eating, he called Brittani. He hoped Brittani would answer the phone because he didn't want to deal with her mom.

She did, "Hello."

"Hey, baby, what you doing?"

"Damien you know my momma is hot with you. I can't believe you tried to put your hand between my legs."

Damien laughed, "Come on girl you should go ahead and give it to me."

"What? I'm only 14 and I told you in the beginning I wasn't going there, Mr. Black."

Damien got mad, "Why, 14 is old enough. Or is it that you just don't love me?"

Brittani deeply sighed, "I can't believe you're trying to pull that card. I do love you, but that has nothing to do with sex. I don't need to have sex with you to prove I love you. But, it would prove that you love me if you could be with me without sex. What you got to say to that, baby."

Damien was very upset now. He thought about his father and how he had told him that he was 11 when he lost his virginity. Damien was 14 and still hadn't. He felt like less of a man and when his father asked him about Brittani he was ashamed. She constantly reminded him that she wasn't going to have sex with him and it angered him greatly.

He couldn't let her see that. He had to keep stringing her along until he got it, "I do love you and I can be with you without sex forever. You just don't understand a man's got needs."

Brittani didn't say anything. Damien continued, "Are you still there?"

"Yes Damien I'm here, and I hear what you're saying but like I told you when we started, I'm not doing it. I'm only 14 and I'm waiting. If you can't handle, then I'm strong enough to let you go. I won't compromise my beliefs for love."

Damien thought, *"Oh no, not the Jesus stuff again. It's time to get off the phone."* Damien replied, "I understand your beliefs. I just wish you could see my side of this."

"I do see your side and they're not matching. Maybe we need to rethink this relationship."

Damien was shocked, "Wait no, that's not the answer." If he told his dad that Brittani had broken up with him, his dad would really think he was a punk. He couldn't allow that.

"I'm sorry, Brittani. I get crazy sometimes. Can we talk about something else?"

Brittani answered, "Sure but it would have to be tomorrow. My mom is telling me to get off the phone and you know how she feels about you."

"Okay, well I can't wait to see you in school tomorrow."

"I can't wait to see you either. Goodnight, Damien."

"Goodnight, Brittani...I love you."

"I love you too, Damien."

He hung up the phone and cursed under his breath. He was never going to get with Brittani, and he knew it. He couldn't talk to his father because he would think less of him. He would have to do something to prove to his father that he was a man like him.

4

This was the worst part of every day for LaJuan. The darkness had covered all of Belmont Heights, and everyone was in their apartments and living their lives. She imagined girls who she went to school with enjoying their evening with their families.

She experienced that peace one night when she spent the night at the house of a friend, who always seemed to have love in her house.

That one night was better than any night LaJuan had experienced since the death of father. When her mother remarried, her life ended. She felt the LaJuan Craig the world knew died that day.

She knew people knew about the abuse, but no one cared to help. No one raised a hand to save her from the hell she was living. The only person that even came up to her was Markus. She could tell Markus cared, probably because he was going through some abuse in his house.

She could hear her mother and stepfather downstairs having fun. She knew they were drinking. She wanted to climb out the window and escape, but she was afraid she would fall.

Suddenly she heard a pounding at the front door. She thought, *"Please be someone to save me! Please!"* Her prayer was answered. It was her aunt on her dad's side. She would come in town on occasion and pick LaJuan up for the weekend. She hoped she could stay with her on a school night so she wouldn't have to deal with her parents.

LaJuan's mom came upstairs, "LaJuan your Aunt Carol is here to pick you up so take your school clothes with you. You won't be coming back until Sunday."

LaJuan was overly excited, but she didn't want to express that excitement to her mom. Instead, she simply said, "Yes, Momma."

LaJuan's mom continued, "Please baby don't tell your aunt what's going on. If you do, they may put your mom in jail. You don't want that do you? You know I love you. I just need some time to get myself together, and then we can escape from here...okay?"

LaJuan was sad. She didn't know whether to believe her mom or not but it was her mother, she had to believe what she was saying. LaJuan said, "I won't tell, Momma. I promise I won't."

She hugged LaJuan tightly, and LaJuan cried. She hated her life, but she couldn't bring herself to hate her mom.

LaJuan quickly grabbed her clothes and sprinted down the stairs. At the foot of the stairs was Aunt Carol and LaJuan was so happy to see her again. For a few days, she would have peace. Nothing bad could happen to her with Aunt Carol.

***

LaJuan's aunt dropped her off at school. She jumped out of her aunt's rental car bouncy and happy. It was Friday, and she didn't have to stay at home the previous night. She made up her mind that this was going to be a great day. Nothing was going to spoil it.

As soon as she got into the hallway, she ran into Damien. He was hanging with his boys, laughing and making fun of anyone who passed by. She knew she would be next. She couldn't stand any of them, especially Damien. She wished he was dead.

Damien smirked, "Well, well, well, look who we have here fellas. Didn't ride in on the bus so what? I'm guessing her boyfriend brought her here? Naw, couldn't be who would date her? I'm betting your pimp brought you here."

Damien and his crew laughed. LaJuan just stared at him and walked by. She wasn't going to let Damien ruin her day. Nothing was going to ruin it.

Once she was by them she smiled, happy that she didn't stoop to his level. Damien shouted, "Let me know when it's my turn to hit that stank."

She heard all of them laugh some more but again she was stronger than that. As much as he might act like he hated her, she knew Damien liked her. He just didn't want to show it to his boys.

But she hated him and wanted nothing to do with him. She knew one day they were going to clash but today wouldn't be that day. Today was Friday and she would spend the weekend with her aunt and have some fun.

***

The last school bell rang signaling it was over for the day, and LaJuan couldn't wait to get to the parking lot. She put her books in her locker and ran. She didn't get 10 feet before she tripped and fell to the ground.

She looked back and saw Damien laughing at her with his friends. He had stuck his foot out and tripped her to the ground. She was angry. Her weekend was about to start, but she couldn't take it anymore.

LaJuan popped up and ran at Damien tackling him to the ground. Damien's boys grabbed her and held her up. Damien jumped up and punched LaJuan in the face and stomach. A teacher came to LaJuan's aid and broke it up. All of them had to go to the office.

The principal separated them and talked to LaJuan first. Her aunt came into the office to sit with LaJuan.

The principal was Diane Davis. She was tough but fair. LaJuan knew she would get suspended no matter what and this was going to be terrible for her because her mother would be angry. Not to mention she would be home alone all day.

Mrs. Davis sat down and looked at LaJuan, "I know you are having a hard school year, LaJuan but I know you can do better than what you are doing. I feel like there is something that you're not telling me. Why did you attack Damien?"

LaJuan said sternly, "He tripped me. I was running to the parking lot to meet my aunt and he stuck his foot out and tripped me on purpose. I took all his harassment all day long but that was it."

Aunt Carol said, "I'm sure LaJuan means to say she's sorry for reacting that way and we hope you will not suspend her from school."

Mrs. Davis replied, "I'm sorry, but that's not an option. She's going to be suspended. I don't tolerate fighting in this school for any reason. Now, LaJuan is there anything else you want to tell me?"

LaJuan was looking down. Her aunt touched her on the shoulder and LaJuan jumped slightly, "No...there's nothing else to tell."

Mrs. Davis nodded her head in disbelief, "Okay, you leave me no choice. You're suspended for five days."

LaJuan gasped, "Five days? You can't do that to me."

Mrs. Davis replied, "I'm sorry but if it's any consolation Damien and those boys will be getting the same five days."

LaJuan shouted, "But Mrs. Davis..."

Her aunt grabbed her by the arm and pulled her out the office. LaJuan was in tears. To her five days was a death sentence but she couldn't tell them why. It was a secret she wasn't allowed to tell.

5

Damien sat in the principal's office confident in himself. He didn't care if he did get suspended. To him, it was a badge of honor, one that his father would take pride in him over.

He was shocked and angry to see his mom come in instead of his father. Rhonda took a seat next to her son and across the desk from Mrs. Davis.

Mrs. Davis said, "Hello, Mrs. Black. I'm sorry you had to come down here for this incident with Damien. He's a good boy, but sometimes he can be trouble, especially when he's around some of his friends."

Rhonda nodded her head in agreement, "What did he do this time?"

Damien looked at his mother with anger. She wasn't supporting him like he knew his father would have.

Mrs. Davis continued, "He got into a fight with a girl at the end of school today, so I'm suspending him for five days."

Rhonda's head dropped. She looked at Damien, "What do you have to say?"

Damien answered, "Nothing."

Rhonda looked in the other direction in shame. She asked, "Is that your family?"

Mrs. Davis smiled, "Yes. That's my husband, he teaches at Chamberlain and my three daughters, Penny, Nya, and Raine."

Rhonda said, "There're beautiful. I know you're proud."

Mrs. Davis answered, "I am very proud. Damien is a good boy, and we can get through his issues. I remember your oldest son, Markus when he came through. He was such an outstanding student, and I know Damien has it in him to be..."

Damien shouted, "Don't compare me to that punk! I'm nothing like him."

Rhonda grabbed him by the arm, "Damien! Don't you talk back to her like that. You have embarrassed me enough today. Come on here boy."

Damien said under his breath, "I wish Dad were here, he would have stood up for me." He walked out the office and to the car.

***

Damien was sitting on his front porch. His mother punished him for getting suspended. Brittani came up to the porch and smiled at him. Damien stood up and hugged her, "Took you long enough."

"What, you should be happy I came after I found out you jumped on a girl. That's weak, Damien."

Damien sat down. He wasn't happy with that comment, "Don't call me weak."

Brittani said sarcastically, "What, you gonna get your boys to hold me down and beat me?"

Damien snapped up and grabbed her by the shoulders, "Don't play with me, Brittani!" He could see the fear in her eyes and slowly let go, "I'm…I'm sorry. I didn't mean that."

Brittani just stood there. Damien hugged her, "I'm sorry…it won't happen again, I promise." She smiled, and Damien thought, *"Dad was right. It does work."*

Brittani said, "You need to talk to someone, Damien. I'm not feeling the way you're acting right now."

Damien said, "You don't know what LaJuan did to me. If you knew what she did, you would understand why we don't like each other."

Brittani replied, "Well I just don't like what I just saw in you. You've changed over the past year. This isn't you."

Damien responded, "You're right baby. There's so much going on in my house and with LaJuan you just don't understand the pressure I feel every day. I mean if it wasn't for you, I don't know what I would do. You keep me centered on what's right and when you're not around I lose it."

Brittani smiled and Damien felt he had her in the palm of his hands, "Now come over here and give me a kiss."

"Okay, but if you put your hand anywhere they don't belong, I'm out of here."

Damien kissed her, and this time he decided to behave. He knew Brittani meant it, and he didn't want to screw up again.

Damien saw his dad come up to the porch. He let go of Brittani and stood there looking at his father. He didn't know what to say.

John said, "Young lady, it's time for you to leave."

Brittani replied, "Yes sir. Bye, Damien."

Damien said meekly, "Bye sweetheart."

Brittani ran off. Damien didn't know what to expect from his father. Would he be happy that he beat up LaJuan or would he be happy that he got suspended from school?

John motioned, "In the house...now." Damien turned and walked in the house. Their apartment front door was in front of the staircase, and the force of the blow to his head was so great it knocked him to his knees. Blood splattered on the steps, and Damien was stunned.

John grabbed Damien by the shirt and punched him in the face several times before his mother threw herself between them. John grabbed her and threw her out the way. He closed the front door so the neighbors wouldn't hear.

He shouted, "Since when did I teach you to need help jumping on a girl. What kind of man are you? You need your boys to hold her down while you beat her! Next time you better do it yourself."

He slapped Damien again, knocking him down again. Markus stood at the top of the steps looking down. John said, "What the hell you looking at? You want some too?"

John walked toward the kitchen, "Where's my dinner?"

Rhonda meekly replied, "It's on the table." She ran over to Damien see how he was doing.

Damien stood up. His mom tried to hold him, but Damien pushed her away and ran up the stairs. He couldn't make eye contact with Markus. He was embarrassed and ashamed. His father thought less of him because his boys held LaJuan while he beat her up. He had to deal with LaJuan.

Damien looked in the mirror as he cleaned up the blood. He felt a little dizzy, but he knew he had to man up. Rhonda asked, "Damien are you all right baby?"

"I'm not a baby. Can't you just leave me alone?"

Rhonda asked, "Why don't you let me help you son? You're my child, and I can't let you bleed to death."

Damien looked at her. Sometimes he despised her meekness. Other times he appreciated it. This was one of the times he appreciated it. He really needed to be cared for by his mom, but he didn't want his dad to think he was a punk.

Damien was overjoyed that his dad went out the door when one of his friends came over. Damien fell into his mother's arms and cried. He saw Markus and Kyanna staring at him, but he didn't care. His father wasn't around, and he could allow his mother to take care of him.

Rhonda rubbed her son's head, took the towel and wiped the blood from his head. She got a bandage and peroxide, cleaned the wound and bandaged it up for Damien.

She asked, "Are you hungry, baby?"

Damien replied, "Yes, ma'am. Thank you, Momma."

Rhonda said, "Son, you don't have to thank me, I'm your mother. You also don't have to be tough for your father. You're a 14 year -old boy who needs love. You try too hard to please your father, and it's taking away the sweet and kind nature I know you have."

Damien just looked down. He knew his mother was right, but he wanted his father's approval. He couldn't understand why but he just did.

Damien went downstairs and ate dinner alone at the table. He was deep in thought about his life and direction it was taking. His mother and Brittani had both told him he was changing. He knew he was changing. He was becoming more like his father, but he couldn't help it. He needed his father's approval.

6

LaJuan sat in the hotel room while her aunt was out getting them some food. LaJuan didn't want to go with her because she wasn't happy about the five-day suspension. She wasn't looking forward to a week at home. Her stepdad would be there alone with her most of the time, and she knew she was going to hate it.

She planned to leave the apartment before her mom left for work and find somewhere to hide out until she came home. At least it would be less violent when her mom was around.

The two most prominent people in her life were gone, and all she had left in life was her mother. Both her father and grandmother were gone. When they were around LaJuan was the happiest girl on the planet, but now she hated her life.

It seemed nothing went her way. She was so lonely that she couldn't stand it. She had no friends. She wanted to leave the hotel, but she didn't want to make her aunt mad and take her back home. That would be the ultimate punishment.

She just decided to stay in the room and wait for her aunt to come back. The phone rang in the room, and LaJuan answered it thinking it was her aunt.

"Hello."

"Hey, LaJuan. I heard you're staying with your aunt this weekend."

She cringed. It was her stepdad, "Why are you calling me? Where's my mom."

"She's in the shower, but I just wanted to hear your voice before she came out. I wanted to be imaging you."

LaJuan slammed the phone down, flopped on the bed and cried. She felt worthless.

***

It was Saturday morning, and LaJuan woke up from a peaceful sleep. Her aunt was still asleep, so she decided to go outside and get some fresh air. She walked out the hotel and took a deep breath. It felt good. This was one of the moments she often cherished. She wasn't with her parents, and there was no threat of abuse.

Next door was an IHOP. She wanted some breakfast, so she went back inside and asked her aunt for some money. She was half asleep and said okay. LaJuan took the money and went to the IHOP.

She went inside, and the hostess sat her at a table where she could see the entrance. After she ordered her food, she saw Brittani come in with her mom and siblings. LaJuan and Brittani got along in school, but LaJuan couldn't understand what she saw in Damien.

Brittani waved at LaJuan and LaJuan smiled and waved back. Surprisingly to LaJuan Brittani came over and sat with LaJuan, "Hey girl, how are you?"

LaJuan smiled trying to be cordial, "Hey Britt. How you doing?"

"I'm good. I didn't think I would run into you here."

"Yeah, I'm staying next door with my aunt. She's in town this weekend. Most of the time she comes and picks me up and lets me stay with her because she knows I hate living at home."

Brittani stared into LaJuan's eyes, "I feel bad for you. I wish there was something I could do."

LaJuan faked a smile, "There's nothing anyone can do. I have four years until I graduate. If I make it, then I'll go far away from here."

Brittani put her hand on LaJuan's hand, "Look, I chastised Damien for what he did to you yesterday. He promised me he wouldn't do it anymore."

LaJuan snapped, "And you believed him?"

"Yeah, I do. At the end of the day, he does love me, and I believe he will change back to the sweet young man I know he can be."

LaJuan nodded her head, "I don't think so. You only see him at certain times. I live two doors down from him. He's a jerk, and he fakes it for you. Damien wants badly to be like his father and that includes beating women. If anyone knows this, I do."

"I can't accept that, LaJuan."

LaJuan smacked her lips, "You will when he does it to you. Markus, Damien's older brother, is nothing like his father but Damien wants to be just like him. He's going to hit you one day and then you'll realize that I was right."

"Okay, we can agree to disagree. Damien would never hit me."

LaJuan smiled as the waitress sat her food down on the table, "I truly hope you're right. I don't think so, but for your sake, I hope you are."

Brittani stood up, "I am. Enjoy your breakfast."

LaJuan delivered another fake smile as Brittani turned and walked away. She knew she was right and one day Damien was going to abuse Brittani. It was only a matter of time before the son became exactly like his father.

LaJuan's aunt came into IHOP and joined her at the table, "You didn't wait for me?"

"Auntie, I thought you were still sleeping."

"Well you woke me up so now I'm up.
Want to do something fun today?"

LaJuan got excited, "Yeah!"

7

Markus, Kyanna, and their mother went to the grocery store. They left Damien and their father at home. Markus knew Damien didn't want to come because he was embarrassed by the events of the last evening. It didn't matter to Markus because they had grown so far apart.

Markus was playing with Kyanna as they were going through the store. Rhonda said, "What am I going to do with the two of you?"

Markus answered, "Keep us, you know you love us."

Kyanna added, "Yeah Mom, what bighead said."

Markus lovingly shoved her, "Who you talkin' 'bout?" He grabbed his baby sister and lifted her up. Kyanna laughed and scream while Rhonda just nodded her head and smiled.

Markus knew she was happy to see them playing and having a good time. They suffer so much at home that it was fun to get out of the house and enjoy some time together even if it was just going to the grocery store.

Markus heard a voice from behind him, "Hey Markus."

He quickly turned and froze, not knowing what to say. Renata turned her head sideways expecting a reply from him.

Kyanna pushed Markus, "Ah, hey Renata, how are you?"

She smiled, and it lit up Markus' insides. He thought he was going to pass out. Renata answered, "I'm doing good, just shopping with my mom." She pointed at her mother and Markus looked. He thought, "Her mom is just as beautiful. Now I see where Renata got it from."

Kyanna said, "I'm Kyanna, bighead's little sister."

Markus snapped, "Shut up girl."

Renata laughed, "Ahhhh, don't be mean she's cute. How old are you?"

"I'm 12. My brother likes..."

Markus put his hand over her mouth, "My sister talks too much. Well, we need to catch up with our mother. It was nice seeing you, Renata."

Renata said, "Hey if you're not busy why don't you come over for dinner tonight? My family is going to be at our apartment. We're celebrating my mom's birthday so you can be my date."

Markus thought he was going to die, "Date? Me and you? Really?"

Renata continued to laugh. Markus didn't know if she was laughing at him or if she was laughing because he was acting so stupid.

She took a step closer to him, and Markus managed to say, "I thought Eddie was your boyfriend."

Renata frowned, "No, who told you that?"

"He did, in the locker room. He says a lot of things about you. I hope they aren't true."

Renata covered her mouth, "Oh my God. I can't stand him. No, he's not my boyfriend, and he never was either so everything he said is not true."

"I didn't believe him. I don't think anyone did. He's a known liar."

Renata smiled, "I'm glad you didn't. Are you coming over tonight?"

He looked over at his mother. Rhonda and Kyanna were both smiling hard. Rhonda said, "It's okay with me."

Markus said, "I'll be there."

"Great, we're starting at six. By the way, I like punctuality." She smiled and walked toward her mother.

Markus stood there not believing what happened. He had to be dreaming. The girl of his dreams just invited him to her apartment for dinner. Rhonda and Kyanna came running over.

Kyanna teased, "Markus got a girlfriend, Markus got a girlfriend!"

Rhonda said, "See how things work out. You thought she didn't like you and look at this...she invited you to her place for dinner. Now you see the goodness of God."

Markus replied, "I just wish he would get us away from dad."

Rhonda put her arm around him, "Come on baby, God will come through for us. I believe He will change John into a true man of God one day."

Markus didn't want to respond. He felt that his dad would never become a man of God. He was evil to him and couldn't imagine him any other way. But for now, things were going great for Markus. He had a date with the girl he has been in love with for the last two years. He thought, *"What am I going to wear!"*

***

It was 4:30 and Markus was tearing through his clothes trying to find the right outfit to wear. Time was his enemy as he was preparing for this, his first date ever in life and it was with the girl he loved from afar.

Damien came in the room, "You're such a little punk. I can't believe you're stressing over a girl like this. They're a dime a dozen."

Markus rolled his eyes at him, "You don't know real love at all."

"Yeah right, real love is when you knock those boots. I know what real love is and you're still a little punk virgin."

Markus looked him square in the eyes, "And I'm proud of it. When I lose mine, it will be with the right person. A person I love and care the world about."

"Wow, you sound like a girl, dude." Damien laughed and walked out the room. Markus knew he could never reach his little brother. His dad had done too much damage. He didn't believe Damien had been sexual with anyone but the fact that he felt the way he did bothered Markus so much.

Markus meant what he said about his virginity. He didn't want to just give it away. In church, he often listened to what people would say on the subject. He had several conversations with his mom, and he knew that unlike many of his friends he cherished his virginity. It was going to go to someone special on a special day, like his wedding night. He hoped Renata would be that special someone.

***

It was 5:30 when someone knocked on the Black's apartment door. Markus was just about dressed and ready. His mom was looking him over when they heard Kyanna, "Markus someone is here for you."

Markus was puzzled. Who would be here for him? He ran downstairs and saw Andra smiling at him.

Markus asked, "Hey, what brings you here?"

Andra answered, "I wanted to give you these."

Markus was truly puzzled now, "You're giving me flowers. I don't understand. You like me or something?"

Andra laughed, "No silly, they are for you to take with you to Renata's tonight. Flowers will go over good, and since it's your first date, I figured I better help you out."

Markus smiled, "Thanks, Andra. I really appreciate it. You think she'll like them?"

"Come on Markus, who knows Renata better than me?"

Markus replied, "I guess you're right about that." Suddenly there was another knock at the door. John shouted, and Andra jumped, "Come in! What the hell is this Union Station?"

Paula walked in, and Markus could see the slight frown on her face. He knew she hated his dad as much as he did.

Markus said, "Hey Paula. What's up?"

Paula said, "Hey Markus, hey, Andra. Here, this is for your date."

"Wow, everyone is helping me out. Thanks. You know she likes chocolate?"

Andra said, "Yep."

Rhonda joined them in the living room. She was clearly elated with the prospect of Markus's first date.

John jumped in the conversation, "Markus I need you to go on a run with me."

Markus was stunned, "But dad, I have to be at Renata's place in a few minutes."

"What did I just say? Tell that girl you'll see her another time."

Rhonda asked, "Why are you doing this? It's his first date with this girl, and he likes her a lot."

John snapped up, "You girls need to leave, and I said Markus I need you to come with me...I mean it now!"

Markus didn't know what to do. He saw Damien in the kitchen laughing. *:"I know he had something to do with this! Nothing ever works out for me."*

Andra gently took the flowers and candy from Markus, "I'll deliver these for you. Don't worry about it, Markus."

They both walked out the apartment. John snatched Markus by the arm to lead him out the back door. Markus stared at his mother, and she was crying. She was more hurt than Markus. He really hated his father now.

***

It was 6:00 and Markus was sitting in his father's car angry. Once again his father had managed to ruin his life. If he wasn't telling him he was good for nothing, he was beating his mother or one of his siblings. He had to get away from him, but he didn't know how and even if he did what would happen to his baby sister. He was old enough to help his sister. He couldn't leave her in that home. Damien wouldn't help her, so he had to be the one to make the sacrifice.

His father came back to the car and got inside. He opened the package he got from the house and rolled up a joint. He eased back in the car, lit it up and inhaled it. John took a deep sigh as he enjoyed the marijuana. Markus rolled down the window.

John sternly said, "Roll that window up."

"I can't stand the smell of that stuff."

John swiped across the seat and hit Markus hard in the chest, "I said roll it up, now!"

Markus rolled up the window. He envisioned ways to kill his father, but he knew that was against the will of God. He couldn't understand why God was making him suffer this life. Instead of enjoying the evening with the girl of his dreams he was stuck in a car with an abusive addict. He felt alone. No one could help him and if they could, they wouldn't. No one ever got involved in these cases. It was the family secret that no one wanted to really know.

John said, "I saved you tonight."

Markus looked at him with pure hatred. He continued, "If you had gone with that girl you would have been destroyed. You see no real woman wants a sissy who shows up at her house with flowers and candy. You gotta be tough, thuggish even. Women respect a man like that. They don't want a punk with flowers.

"That's not true."

"Don't tell me, boy. I'm the man here, and you don't know squat. Those girls are turning you into a sissy. You need to hang out with boys like Cleveland and Eddie. They know how to treat a girl. You don't see them showing up with flowers to a girl's house."

Markus snickered, "Eddie's nothing but a liar. He says a lot of things about girls and none of them are true."

"Awwww what, he said something about your little hussy? I bet he nailed it and you punked out."

Markus grew even angrier, "He hasn't touched Renata. He's a liar."

John laughed loudly. It filled the car, "You're jealous because he hit it and you can't. I can't believe you're my son. What a sissy."

Markus didn't want to argue with him. He really hated him, and now he disrespected the girl he loved, but he is bigger and stronger. Markus couldn't take him if he tried.

John started the car up, and they drove off to another part of town. He parked the car near some apartments and got out, "Stay here. I'll be right back."

Markus answered, "Okay." Then he said under his breath, "Sure you will."

His father had deliberately kept him from spending time with Renata, and now he was stuck in the car in some apartment complex far away from the projects. He wondered if his dad thought he was a complete idiot. Markus knew what he was doing inside. He was cheating on his mom...again.

Markus thought out loud, *"I will never be the man he is, never."*

He spotted a phone booth at the end of the parking lot. He reached into his pocket and pulled out some change. He had enough to make one call. He didn't have Renata's number, but he had Paula and Andra's number. He would call Andra since she was Renata's best friend.

He got out the car and ran down the street to the payphone and called Andra.

The phone rang, and he prayed she would answer. However, it was her mom, "Hello."

Markus answered, "Hello, may I speak to Andra?"

Her mom said, "Hold on." He heard her call out for Andra. That was a good sign. At least he would be able to talk to her and find out how Renata took the news. He thought, *"She probably wants nothing to do with now."*

Suddenly the Andra was there, "Hello."

Markus excitedly said, "Hello, hey Andra this is Markus."

"Hey Markus, I'm sorry, but I can't stand your dad. He's a jerk."

Markus couldn't stand him either, "I know what you mean, and you don't have to apologize for it. Is Renata mad?"

"She is but not at you. I told her the whole story and she said if you call or something to tell you to come to her church tomorrow. She goes to Saint Matthews on Lake. You can walk there."

Markus was so happy, "I'll be there. What time do they start?"

"I think it's at 11, but I'm not sure. Just be there. You can make this right."

Markus was afraid to ask but he did, "Andra, does she like me...really?"

"What's not to like Markus? You're handsome, smart and a really good guy. You one of the ones who respect girls and Renata is big on that. She told me what you said about Eddie. He's a jerk, and she would never go out with him so don't believe anything he has to say."

"I already learned not to believe him. Cleveland caught him in so many lies it's a shame. I will be at church tomorrow. Thanks, Andra."

"You're welcome. Bye, Markus."

"Bye, Andra."

He hung up the phone and happily ran back to the car. So his dad might have stopped him from going to the dinner, but he won't stop him from seeing Renata at church. He won't even tell him that he's going to church. He won't tell anyone.

He got back to the car and waited for his dad to return from his adulterous rendezvous.

***

Markus and his dad got home around midnight. He had fallen asleep in the car waiting for his dad, so he was wide awake now. His mom was still awake when he got home. Thankfully his dad just went upstairs and got in the bed. Markus guessed he didn't need mom because he had spent time with his side chick.

Markus sat on the couch while his mother sat in the chair. She looked at him with sorrowful eyes. Markus loved his mother. When he hurt, she felt his pain. Rhonda softly said to him, "That girl called."

Markus perked up, "She did?"

Rhonda got up and went to sit by Markus. She put her arm around him, "Yes she did, and she asked if it was okay for you to go to Saint Matthews tomorrow. Of course, I said 'yes.'"

"Wow, I talked to her best friend and she told me the same thing. Please don't tell anyone else. Dad will just stop me from going again. He said I was a sissy."

She hugged him tightly, "Don't you believe that! You are a good boy and the girls like you because you are good."

"He said only sissies bring flowers and candy to girls and that girls like tough, thuggish guys."

Rhonda hugged him tighter, "Don't you believe that. Don't ever mention this or he'll kill me but your dad was the consummate gentlemen. When we were dating, he brought me flowers, candy and gave me cards. That mess about losing his virginity at 11 is also a lie. We were 19, and we both lost it together."

"Your dad was nothing like the man you see today. When he lost his job and couldn't care for his family, the world harden him. He blamed me for getting pregnant and him not getting into the music business. Since then he became this abusive man. I know he can change back to the loving man. I just know it."

Markus looked his mother deep in the eyes, "I don't think he will ever change momma."

Rhonda smiled, "I do. Please don't tell anyone what I told you. He would lose his mind if he found out I told that."

Markus hugged her tightly, "I will never give him reason to hurt you, Momma."

Rhonda smiled some more, "I know you won't son. Now I'd better get some sleep. I think I'm going to church tomorrow too."

"Good night, Momma."

"Good night son."

Markus sat on the couch for a few more hours watching TV and praying that his meeting with Renata would go well. He didn't have the flowers and candy, but he could make a card to give to her at service. Then he reasoned that would be too stupid.

8

Markus jumped up and went into the bathroom before anyone else got up. He wanted to get dressed and ready for church. He actually liked going to church, but this service would be different. This time he would see Renata and she wasn't mad at him for not coming to dinner.

When he came out the bathroom, his mom was standing there smiling. She was happy for him. She whispered, "You excited?"

Markus whispered back, "Yeah." He ran into the room and quickly put on his church clothes. He wanted to get dressed, ready and out of the house before his dad got up.

Markus ran downstairs and made himself some cereal. He quickly ate it all and dashed out the back door. Before he did, he heard Damien yell, "Where you going?"

Markus said, "None of your business."

***

Markus had two hours before service started. He went to his best friend's house and knocked on the door.

Cleveland came to the door and let him in, "What's up dude? It's nine in the morning."

"Yeah I know. I needed somewhere to hang until about 10:45. I'm going to Renata's church, and I don't want my dad to stop me this time."

Cleveland asked, "This time? He stopped you before?"

"Yeah yesterday I was supposed to go to her place for dinner with her family, and he made me go with him instead. He can be such a jerk."

Cleveland nodded his head, "Man you got it bad, bro."

"He told me he saved me from being a sissy because Andra and Paula gave me flowers and candy to give Renata."

Cleveland laughed, "Dude, tell me you weren't going to do that? You can't go out like that, man. Real men don't do that stuff. Man, the minute you do that she'll know she got you whipped. You don't want to be whipped."

"I don't see anything wrong with it, especially if a girl likes flowers and candy. You're just showing her that you like her and you care about her enough to give her something you know she'll appreciate."

Cleveland said, "I can respect that if it gets you some." He laughed, and Markus nodded his head in disbelief.

Markus replied, "It's not just about 'getting some.' It's about love...real love and real love is more than sex."

"Says the virgin."

"Okay, what's on TV? I got two hours to sit here so let's talk about something else."

Cleveland said, "Yeah, you gonna miss the game today."

"Oh well."

"Dang, you're whipped."

***

Markus got to the church just before 11. He sat in the back so he could see Renata when she came in the sanctuary. He saw his dad, mom, Damien and Kyanna come in a few minutes after him. He hoped and prayed that they wouldn't sit near him, but he saw Kyanna point at him.

John looked at him angrily. Markus knew he wouldn't act up in the house of the Lord. One thing Markus learned about his life is that the things that happened to them always happened when people weren't around to witness it. That's why he hated nights and weekends in his house.

The service was almost halfway done, and Renata wasn't there. The longer it went on, the more sad Markus became. Again he couldn't believe his luck. He questioned if God even cared in the least about him.

When the service was over a little girl came up to Markus and handed him a folded piece of paper. She was about nine years old, and Markus didn't know who she was. He unfolded the note and read it.

"Markus, I'm sorry I wasn't at church today. I must have eaten something that disagreed with my stomach. I was very sick this morning. I hope to get better before school tomorrow. Since we're in lunch together, maybe we can eat together and talk. Thinking of you, Renata"

Markus leaned down to the little girl, "Is this from your sister?"

"Yes. She likes you."

He smiled, "Tell her I would be glad to have lunch with her tomorrow and that I hope she feels better."

"Okay."

"Hey, what's your name?"

"Tiffani." She ran away to some adults that Markus reasoned were Renata's parents.

Damien was behind Markus, "So you can't get someone your age so now you going with nine-year-olds. Wow, what a punk." He laughed, but Markus didn't pay him any attention.

Damien continued, "You might as well get ready because dad was upset you weren't at home this morning. He's going to pile drive your butt."

Markus said, "You know Damien, I don't understand why you enjoy what he does to us so much, but I don't even care what he does to me anymore. One day I'm going to be free of him, and I'm going to start a business that will stop monsters like him...and you."

Markus pushed passed his brother and ran over to his little sister. He hugged her, and she hugged him back. Markus cared so much for his little sister and his mom, but his relationship with Damien was headed in the opposite direction.

John rolled his eyes at Markus. Markus couldn't believe how he was looking at him and still laughing and joking with the pastor. He was truly the emancipation of evil.

On the way home, John didn't say a word in the car. Kyanna talked almost the entire trip home while everyone else just listened. Markus thought she had a beautiful spirit. He prayed that his father wouldn't take it away.

When they got in the house, John closed the wood door and removed his belt. He grabbed Markus by the arm yanked him to the floor. Kyanna started to cry. John shouted, "Shut up before I give you some too!"

John started hitting Markus with the belt. He didn't care where the belt landed he just swung with all his might. Markus turned on his back, and the hit sounded louder than the one before it.

Kyanna screamed. John went to her, "Scream again, and you'll get some."

Markus pleaded, "Don't Kyanna, I'll be okay." He saw his mom covering her mouth and protecting Kyanna. Damien was nowhere to be seen.

After a minute of more hits John grabbed Markus and pulled him up from the floor, "I told you not to go see that heifer didn't I. You want to be a sissy, I'll make you a sissy."

He pushed Markus in the chair and grabbed Rhonda's purse. Rhonda asked, "What you are doing? Don't..."

John pointed at her, "Don't get me started on you." He pulled out some lipstick, grabbed Markus and started painting the lipstick on him.

Rhonda said, "Stop! Stop it!"

The backhand slap was so forceful that it knocked both Rhonda and Kyanna to the ground. Markus tried to go help his mom and John flung him to the floor. He towered over them, daring any of them to move. Rhonda covered Kyanna to protect her, and Markus stared coldly at him.

"You want some of me, don't you boy. I can see it in your eyes. You think you can take me? Come on get up and be a man."

Rhonda meekly said, "Don't Markus...please."

John said, "Yeah that's what I thought." He turned and headed out the front door. Markus got up and went to his mom. She quickly wiped the lipstick off of her son and held him tight.

Kyanna was crying. Markus grabbed his baby sister and held her tightly. He glanced up, and Damien was standing on the stairs. He looked coldly at all of them and then went out the front after his dad.

It was clear to Markus that the family was divided. From that point on he didn't care what happened to him, but he was going to protect his mom and sister. He wasn't going to let that monster hurt them anymore.

9

LaJuan had a great day and a great weekend hanging out with her auntie, but now it was ending. She was packing her things to go back to Belmont Heights. A place she had come to hate because of what it represented. To her, it was a place of abuse, and now she was going to be suspended and home every day.

She slowly walked down the sidewalk with her auntie. She saw Brittani talking with some other girls. She rationalized that she was waiting on Damien to come outside. She thought Brittani was stupid for dating Damien and one day she would see for herself.

Before she got to the door, her mom came running out and hugged her, "My baby! I'm so happy to see you again. I pray you had a great time with your aunt."

"I did mom."

"Well, that is awesome. I am glad you're home. I want us to make some smores tonight. How does that sound?"

"Sounds good, Mom."

LaJuan's Aunt Carol said, "You know she's suspended for the week right?"

Deborah Jacobs paused, "I do. The school called Friday. What did you do this time LaJuan?"

LaJuan looked at her with anger, "Why do you blame me? He tripped me, and I defended myself. Then three of them jumped me and you blame me."

Deborah said, "Did you tell that principal what happened?"

LaJuan replied, "Yes and she still suspended me."

Kayla chimed in, "She didn't want to hear it, Deborah. She just punished all the kids the same. The facts didn't mean anything."

Deborah said, "Okay, I'm going down to that school tomorrow and handle it. Go on in the house LaJuan."

LaJuan didn't move. She meekly asked, "Is Donnie in there?"

Deborah got angry, "Don't start. He isn't doing anything to you, and you need to stop lying! No, he's not home yet."

LaJuan stormed off. When she got in the house, she ran to her room and blocked the door. She knew it wouldn't stop him from getting in, but she hoped it would make enough noise that her mom would hear it.

She looked out the window and saw her mom and aunt arguing. She believed her aunt knew what was going on with her but she wouldn't help. LaJuan wasn't surprised no one wanted to confront the family secret.

LaJuan thought about how amazing it was that everyone in her family and probably everyone in the neighborhood knew what was happening to her but no one wanted to talk about it, and they certainly didn't want to help. No one wanted to confront it. She was so alone.

After having such a great weekend, she couldn't imagine suffering through a horrible Sunday night. She decided to contact her old cousin and see if he had some heroin. She used it once, and she liked the fact that she couldn't feel a thing. She made the call.

***

LaJuan's cousin had come for her, and she had the heroin in her room. If her stepdad came home, she would use it to take herself to another place, a place away from Belmont Heights.

She sat in her room and imagined ways that she could kill the object of her abuse. She didn't blame her mom. She really thought she didn't know what was going on with her. It was either that or like everyone else she had her head in the sand.

She heard the front door. She shuddered at the sound. She wished she had a knife or a gun to end her misery. If she was dead, he couldn't hurt her anymore.

She heard her mom coming up the steps. She tried to open the door but the chair stopped her from coming in, and she yelled, "Open this door girl!"

LaJuan got up and moved the chair. Deborah came in the room, "I'm going with Donnie's sister to the jail. It seems Donnie got arrested. Will you be okay here by yourself?"

LaJuan was elated, "Yeah I'll be fine, Momma."

Deborah turned and quickly walked back downstairs. When LaJuan heard the door close she almost shouted with joy. She hid the drugs under her mattress and rested calmly on her bed. She would have another night of peace.

***

LaJuan walked into the principal's office with her mom. She had seen her mom mad before but she was really mad this time. Most of the time she was only mad at her, but this time she was mad at the principal. LaJuan was curious to see how this would play out.

In the office, they sat down in front of Mrs. Davis's desk. Pictures of her family lined the walls and her desk. LaJuan admired the fact that she was proud of her family but at the same time she hated it. She hated her daughters because they didn't know the pain that she knew. They would never know the pain that she knew.

Mrs. Davis started, "As you know LaJuan was caught fighting last Friday after school. No matter what the circumstances fighting will not be tolerated in this school. So I know you're upset..."

"You don't know me at all Mrs. Davis. Let's get that straight first. My daughter is being bullied at this school, and three boys beat her, but she gets the same punishment they did? That's not right. I don't care if she did fight, that Damien boy tripped her first. She should not be punished the same!"

Mrs. Davis politely continued, "I understand you're upset, but my rule is no fighting at all, no matter the circumstance. Since LaJuan was tripped, she should have reported that to a teacher and not taken matters into her own hands."

Deborah replied, "My daughter is bullied here daily, and if you don't reduce her punishment I will be forced to report your lack of support for her to the county school board."

Mrs. Davis looked sternly at Deborah, "Then maybe we should. Because I believe there are problems with LaJuan. Problems she's keeping inside...problems that emanate from home. I've attempted to get her to talk about it but she won't. So maybe the county should become involved."

LaJuan was happy. She thought, *"Yes please get them involved. Somebody help me!"* She didn't want to make eye contact with Mrs. Davis, so she looked at the pictures of her family instead. They looked so happy that it made LaJuan sick.

Deborah stood up, "Let's go LaJuan."

Mrs. Davis stood up, "I'm going to find out what's going on Mrs. Craig. This isn't over."

Deborah turned around and firmly stated, "Stay out of my family's business. You got your family leave mine alone."

LaJuan looked at Mrs. Davis with pleading eyes and followed her mother out the office. She still has no help, but maybe Mrs. Davis will come to her aid at some point before it was too late.

10

Markus was up bright and early. Today had to be the day. He missed out on spending time with Renata on Saturday and Sunday so today should be the day. It had to be the day. He prayed that she was feeling better and would be at school. He didn't want to wait another day.

He finished his breakfast and headed out the front door when Kyanna met him and hugged him, "Good luck big brother!"

"Thanks, little sister."

Damien pushed passed them and went into the kitchen. Markus heard him call him a 'punk' under his breath. Markus was immune to his comments at this point.

He headed out the door and to the bus stop. He ran into Paula and Shelia on the way.

"Hey, ladies. How you guys doing?"

Paula answered, "Good. How was church?"

Shelia said, "Hey Markus."

Markus answered, "Hey, Shelia. Church was good, but Renata didn't come. She was sick."

Shelia replied, "Really? I saw her yesterday by the basketball court. She must have been feeling better."

Markus said, "Must have." He had that pit in his stomach. Maybe Renata wasn't true to him. Maybe she was just playing around with him. He thought, *"Why did she have to say that?"*

They got to the bus stop, and Renata was talking to Andra and Eddie. *"Why did he have to be there? Nothing is going right again."* He didn't know if he should go over to her or not. He looked in her direction, but she didn't look at him. Thankfully the bus pulling up and he wouldn't have to decide.

Everyone got on the bus, and Renata was sitting alone. Markus was shocked she was alone. Renata smiled at him, and he calmly walked to the seat and sat down. Flies ran throughout Markus' stomach.

Renata said, "Sorry about church."

Markus replied, "No problem. I guess you got better."

Renata responded, "Yeah I started to feel better later, and I even went down to the basketball court for a little while. I was kind of hoping you were there."

Markus smiled inside. She wasn't playing around with him. He asked, "So are we still on for lunch?"

Renata smiled, "Oh yeah. You buying, right?"

They both laughed knowing they both don't have to pay for lunch. Markus answered, "Oh course sweetheart I got...I'm sorry I didn't mean to say that."

Renata threw her head back laughing, "It's okay. I like it. Oh, yeah thanks for the flowers and candy! That was so sweet."

"You liked them?"

"Of course I did. What girl wouldn't like receiving flowers and candy? That's what's wrong with most boys they don't think it's mainly to give flowers and candy. As a woman, I love it. That was big points."

Markus couldn't believe it. When he thought everything would go wrong again, it was going right. He hadn't felt this before in his life. His life had been so miserable to this point. Even the day before was horrible with the beating he took from his dad. But today, this one conversation with the girl of his dreams had erased everything.

He didn't want the bus trip to Chamberlain to end, but it slowly did. They got off the bus, and he walked her to class, "Well I will see you at lunch, Miss Smith."

"Why yes you will, Mr. Black. I can't wait to continue our conversation."

Markus smiled hard, "I can't wait to finish it either. Bye, Renata."

"Bye, Markus." Her smile was so bright and beautiful. He knew he wasn't going to be able to concentrate in class at all. He knew he was only going to be thinking of Renata.

***

Markus got to the cafeteria as quick as he could, but he didn't beat Renata there. She was standing there looking as beautiful as ever to Markus. He walked up to her, "Hey, I was trying to beat you here!"

She laughed. When she laughed it made every pain, he might be feeling go away. She said, "Why, it's not a race?"

"I don't know. I just feel like the man should be the one waiting on the woman and not the other way around. I guess I'm crazy like that."

"That's not crazy, that's actually very sweet and gentlemanly. So what are you having the lasagna or the lasagna?"

Markus laughed, "I will have the lasagna, and you?"

"I guess I'll have the lasagna too." They both laughed. She made him feel so comfortable. He felt so confident and relaxed being around her now. They chose a seat away from everyone else. Markus wanted to talk alone and not be disturbed by anyone.

Renata said, "I hear so much about your dad from Paula and Shelia, is he really that bad."

Markus didn't want to talk about that, but he didn't want to be rude, "He's worse than that. I really don't want to talk about my family."

Renata looked down, "I hope one day that you feel comfortable talking to me about it. If we're going down this road, I want there to be no secrets between us."

Markus looked her in the eyes. He could tell she was sincere. She wanted to go down that road with him, and she was serious. He answered, "Somehow I know that I will tell you everything and there won't be any secrets between us."

Markus felt brave he decided to ask her if they were in a relationship now. He didn't know how that was done because he was not experienced in the area. He knew he wanted to be with her and no one else, but he didn't know if she felt the same. He decided to ask.

"Renata…"

"Hey, girl, what you doing over here in the corner? Hey, Markus", Andra interrupted him before he could ask the question. He was disappointed but tried not to show it.

Renata answered, "We were trying to have a nice quiet lunch and some conversation. Know what I mean?"

Andra put her hand up and laughed, "Oh excuse me! I'll be on my way. Bye y'all."

They both smiled and waved. Markus built up his courage again, but the bell rang. He couldn't believe it. They gathered their items and headed to their next class.

Markus walked Renata to her class, and he decided to ask, but she spoke first, "Is there something you want to ask me, Markus? I mean you were going to say something before Andra interrupted."

"Yes, I did. Are we in a relationship? I'm not sure how these things work."

Renata smiled and said, "You're supposed to ask me if I want to be in a relationship with you."

Markus asked, "Renata, will you be my girlfriend?"

Renata answered, "I'll think about it...sweetie." She winked at him and walked in her class.

She didn't say 'yes,' but she didn't say 'no' either. He was excited. He almost ran to class believing she was going to say 'yes' and be his girlfriend. This was his best day ever.

11

School was finally over, and Markus couldn't wait to get to the bus. He watched the clock all day, even trying to make it move faster. When he got to the bus, his heart dropped. Paul, a star on the school's basketball team, was sitting with Renata. He started to sit up front so he wouldn't have to see or hear what they were talking about. He almost didn't notice the look of anger on her face.

Renata motioned for him to come to her and he did. When he got to her seat, Renata said, "Move Paul, I want Markus to sit with me."

Paul said, "What, you want him over me? Come on baby let me talk to you. You know I'm the better choice."

Markus didn't know what to say, should he intervene or not? He didn't have to because Renata stood up, "Move out the way, Paul."

The bus driver asked, "What's going on back there?"

Paul replied, "Nothing." He looked at Renata, "You're not even worth the trouble."

Paul rolled his eyes at Markus. Everyone was waiting with anticipation to see what was going to happen. Renata sat back down and took Markus' hand, "Come on Markus don't buy into that."

Her voice was soft and calming. It made Markus feel special. Her eyes were pleading with him not to cause any trouble. She genuinely cared about him, and he knew it.

Markus sat down and heard the other guys laughing at comments being made by Paul. He didn't care. He had the girl he wanted, and she clearly liked him. In the past, he was intimidated by the athletes, but today Renata showed him that he mattered more to her than they did.

He looked at her, and she was looking at him. She said, "I'm sorry."

Markus replied, "You have nothing to be sorry about. It's cool."

Renata asked, "You wanna move?"
Markus didn't want to move because it would say that they intimidated him. He wanted to show that he wasn't scared of them. After all, he had taken beatings from his dad, and none of these guys were stronger than him.

Renata continued, "Let's move. I don't want to sit here."

Markus got up and led her to a seat closer to the front of the bus. He chose to move because his girl wasn't comfortable, not because Paul scared him.

Renata sat down and touched Markus' arm, "Now that's better."

Markus couldn't be any happier. Every time he thought things were turning bad they weren't. He decided to ask, "Have you thought about my question?"

She laughed, "Markus it's only been a few hours."

Markus said, "Well, it doesn't hurt to check does it?"

"No it doesn't, but you know what...I have thought about it, and we clearly seem like the right combination." She smiled at him, and he could hardly contain himself. He asked, "Sooooo..."

"Okay Markus, I'll give you a chance."

Markus couldn't believe it. Did she just agree to be his girlfriend...really? He asked quietly, "So you're my girlfriend?"

She rubbed his shoulder, "Yes."

Markus was clearly excited, but he realized he had no idea how to be a boyfriend. He took her hand and held it. It was the greatest feeling he ever felt in his life.

She whispered in his ear, "No sex until we're married!"

Sex was the farthest thing from his mind. All he cared about was being her boyfriend. Markus said, "Okay. But I'm your boyfriend right?"

She giggled and laid her head on his shoulder, "Yes."

Markus wanted to stand up and announce it to the bus, but instead, he laid his head on hers and enjoyed the moment.

Andra said, "Isn't that so cute. Does this mean you guys are a couple now?"

Renata gave a 'thumbs up', and Markus realized he couldn't be any happier than he was at that very moment. His life no longer sucked.

***

Markus walked Renata home, and she kissed him on the cheek. He had never been kissed at all except for the kisses his mom gave him. He didn't want to wash that cheek.

He dreaded getting home because he didn't want to have his day turn horrible. It usually went from bad to worst but today was a great day, and he didn't want to see the worst.

He slowly walked in the house, and his dad was sitting in his favorite chair like he was some kind of king. Markus wanted to stay focused on Renata and not let the hate he felt for his father ruin anything. He spoke, "Hi, Dad."

"Hey, how was school?"

The question shocked Markus. His dad never cared about his day. He answered, "It was great."

His dad didn't acknowledge his response. Markus went into the kitchen where his mom and sister were sitting. Kyanna had her head down, and Rhonda looked as though she had been crying. Markus felt something was wrong.

"Hey shrimp, what's wrong cat got your..." He pulled her head back and saw the bruise on her cheek. He was angry. He turned toward his father, but his mother grabbed him. She pleads, "Don't ...please, he calmed down for now. Let it end there."

Markus turned and hugged his little sister. She laid her head on his shoulder and sniffled. Markus knew she was afraid to cry because his father would come in and beat her some more. He hated him.

***

It was late in the evening when the phone rang. Rhonda answered it, "Hello."

"Hello, may I speak to Markus please."

Rhonda smiled, "You sure can. I'll tell him you're on the phone."

Rhonda motioned to Markus that the phone was for him. He rushed over to it. He could tell it was her by the way his mom's face lit up.

"Hey, how are you?"

"I'm good. My mom and I were talking, and she wants you to come over for dinner tomorrow. She wasn't happy that you missed the dinner Saturday."

Markus was excited, "I sure can, and this time I'll make sure nothing comes up. Okay."

"Do your best sweetie."

Markus' face lit up after hearing Renata call him 'sweetie,' "I will honey. You know I've never used that word before."

She laughed, "Well you better not use it on anyone else, or I'll bop you a good one."

He laughed, "You got it. Hey, I have a question for you."

"Okay, what?"

"You said you like super heroes right?"

"Yeah."

"Who would win, Superman or Wonder Woman?"

She laughed, "You're kidding right, you know Wonder Woman would kick Superman's behind. She has the magic lasso and can match his power and strength."

"No baby, you got it wrong Superman would beat her down!"

Renata laughed even more, "You are funny. Superman can't handle magic and Wonder Woman has beaten him before. So, baby, Wonder Woman would kick...his...behind!"

"Oh, I guess we're going to have to agree to disagree on this one. But you're wrong honey."

"Wow, two honeys in one conversation. You're gaining your confidence."

Markus was gaining his confidence, and he owed it to Renata. He noticed everyone in the living room was watching him smile and enjoy his conversation. He was glad his dad wasn't there. He turned away from them and whispered, "The whole room is watching me."

Renata said, "Really, are they happy for you?"

"Yeah my mom and sister are, but I don't think my brother is happy. My dad has influenced him to the point where our opinion on women is as wide as the Grand Canyon."

"That's too bad because you got it right and if he's that far off from you, then I feel for him and the women he dates."

"So do I." Markus heard his dad coming down the stairs, "I have to go. I don't want to talk around my dad."

"Okay, well I'll talk to you tomorrow at school sweetie."

"You better. Goodnight baby."

"Goodnight Markus. Sleep well sweetie."

He hung up the phone on the highest high he had ever experienced in his life. His dad sat down in the living room, and Markus felt the atmosphere in the living room change for the worst.

He got up to go upstairs, and his dad sternly said, "Where you going?"

Markus answered, "Upstairs to do some reading."

John replied, "Sit down. We're going to watch TV as a family."

Markus hated him, but he noticed the pleading in his mom's eyes and decided to just comply. He would watch TV with them, but his mind would be elsewhere.

12

LaJuan was lying in bed hearing the screaming downstairs. Hearing mom and stepdad were at it again and she knew this was not going to be a good night. She ingested the heroin, and the effects were starting to take control.

The euphoria made her feel so good that nothing around her stressed her. The arguing downstairs sounded far off and even at times funny to her. She just laid there and imagined she was somewhere else.

She didn't know how long it had been since she ingested the drugs before her room door opened. The chair didn't block the person entering her room. She heard her mom shout, "Come here?" *"Was she talking to me? I'm so high I don't even know!"* She just laughed and saw the figure leave her room. She laughed even more.

More time went by, and LaJuan had dosed off to sleep. She woke up when she realized that the sensation she was feeling was someone rubbing her hair.

She jumped at first, and then she realized that it was her mom. She asked, "Mom?"

Her mom just smiled and said, "Go back to sleep baby. It's okay, you can sleep comfortably tonight."

LaJuan was still high, but she knew that meant her mom knew what was happening. She knew what her stepfather was doing to her at night. She became angry because she knew but wouldn't stop it.

She wondered what her mom had done on this night that prevented him from coming into her room. She hoped she had killed him.

***

The morning sun plastered across her face and woke her up. She didn't have to go to school, so she took her time and tried to recover from her drug induced state before she got up.

She remembered her mom coming into the room and telling her she would have a comfortable night's sleep. She was right she did sleep comfortable, but now the anger returned.

If her mom knew what was happening to her why did she always call her a liar? What made her even angrier was that she didn't do anything about it.

LaJuan slowly got up and looked in the mirror. She hated herself. She felt used and worthless. She didn't like the drugs, but they took her away from her problems. It made the abuse easier for her to get through. If her cousin ever stopped coming through for her, she wouldn't know what to do.

She came out of her room and stopped in her tracks. Her stepdad was standing there. He looked her up and down. LaJuan tightened her bathrobe and pushed pass him to the bathroom. She quickly locked the door and stepped back, afraid the door would be kicked down.

She ran the bath water and heard her parents arguing some more. She heard her mother threaten to leave. Then she heard them physically fighting. She ran out the bathroom and down the stairs.

Her stepfather was on top of her mom slapping her repeatedly. LaJuan jumped on top of him, and he easily threw her off of him.

He then walked over to her grabbed her by the collar and punched LaJuan in the face. She was dazed, but she could see him beat her mother even more. She heard her mother beg for her life before she passed out.

***

She wasn't sure what time it was but when she came to she saw her mom standing in the mirror applying makeup to her face. LaJuan sat up and asked, "Mom...are you okay?"

Her mom turned and walked over to her, "Hey baby. I'm fine. I'm just getting ready to go to work."

"Mom, why do you let him do this to us? Leave him!"

"Baby, without his income how could we survive? I can't leave him."

LaJuan shouted, "You know what he's..."

Her mom put her hand over LaJuan's mouth, "It's going to be okay baby. It will."

LaJuan slammed her hand on the mattress, got up and stormed out the room. In her room, she looked in the mirror and said to herself, *"I won't be a victim anymore! I don't care what happens to me, I'm not going to be like my mom. It ends today!"*

LaJuan's mom came in the room, "Honey, get dressed and come to work with me. It'll be fun."

LaJuan answered, "Okay, Momma."

She quickly got washed up and dressed. The two left for her mom's job and away from her stepdad. LaJuan spent the entire day thinking of ways to ensure her abuse would end.

13

Damien was bored at home. He had a few dollars on him, and he decided to go get him a Cuban sandwich. He walked into the store and saw LaJuan ordering Cuban sandwiches. He snarled at her and she returned the look.

Damien said, "You looking ugly as usual."

LaJuan replied, "Go to Hell, Damien."

Damien laughed, "It's your fault I'm not in school with my friends and my girl."

"Lucky for her, maybe she'll find someone better for her without you around."

Damien said, "I hate you."

LaJuan laughed, "Really...I think you dream of being with me. You always talk about me because you want me so badly."

"In your dreams."

"No in yours." She laughed some more as she took her sandwiches and walked out the store.

Deep inside Damien felt she was right. He did like her and hated the fact that she didn't like him. He didn't know why he liked her but he did and that was something he would never admit to anyone.

Damien got his sandwich and sat down outside to eat. Cuban sandwiches were a delicacy in Belmont Heights, so Damien cherished the moment. Halfway through his meal two men in suits pulled up, got out their vehicle and sat down with Damien.

Damien was scared. He thought they were the police. One man did all the talking, "Hi Damien. How are you?"

Damien was puzzled, "How do you know me?"

The man answered, "Oh we know a lot about you young man. We know you got musical talent and we want to help you."

Damien didn't know what to do. His instinct told him to run, but the opportunity to get into music made him stay, "How do you know that and why would you help me?"

"Oh, we know a great deal about you, Damien. We've been watching your growth and trust me when I say we're excited about your future."

He continued, "You see we just came here today to let you know that we are here to help you. Take this card and if you need anything give us a call."

Damien took the card. It didn't have a name on it just a number and company name of 'Fresh City Records.' Damien asked, "What is 'Fresh City Records'? I haven't heard of it."

"It's our label. We haven't officially came out yet but in time we will, and you will be a prominent figure in our company." He eased up to Damien, "But you have to learn to get along with LaJuan."

Damien asked, "LaJuan, what does she have to do with this?"

"LaJuan is important to us as well, and we can't have the two of you hating each other. So you need to stop bullying her and be her friend. That is if you want to be big in the music business and earn more money than you can spend."

Damien was excited, "More money than I can spend?"

"Yes." The two men stood up, "Work it out with her and become her friend."

Damien said, "For more money than I can spend, I'll be anybody's friend!"

"Good." The men got back into their vehicle and drove off. Damien never got names from the men, but he had the business card, and he would never lose it. He finished his food and rushed home to hide the card.

14

LaJuan was sitting in the maintenance office of Young Junior High School. Her mom was somewhere in the school cleaning. She enjoyed every bite of her Cuban sandwich and was almost done when two men walked in the room.

A chill ran up LaJuan's back. She didn't know what to do. They had her cornered in the room, and she had no way out.

One man stood at the door while the other sat down next to her, "Hi LaJuan."

LaJuan didn't know this man and she didn't know how he knew her, "How do you know me?"

"We've been watching you for a while, and we know what you've been going through for the past few years. We also know what you're planning to do."

LaJuan was scared. How could they know what she was planning? She wasn't even sure what she was going to do, but she knew she wasn't going to be a victim anymore.

The man continued, "When you take that step we will be there to help you." He smiled, but his smile didn't make LaJuan feel good. It scared her more. His smile was cold, eerie and chilling. LaJuan just sat there and watched them get up and leave.

Before they left the man slowly turned and said, "Remember we'll be there for you when you need us."

They left, and LaJuan sat there wondering what that was all about. A few minutes went by, and her mom came back in the office. She asked, "Hey baby, how was your sandwich?"

"It was good, Mom." She wondered if she should tell her about the men but reasoned that she shouldn't. It was a meeting that you don't share with anyone.

Her mom said, "Well I'm starving, and I can't wait to eat mine." She sat down, prayed over her food and began to eat.

LaJuan just sat there and thought about the men. She continued to ask herself how they could know what she was going to do when she didn't know herself.

***

LaJuan was walking home with her mom. They lived near the school, so it was an easy walk for them. She saw Damien sitting on his porch.

He ran over to her, and she got on the defensive, "Leave me alone Damien."

LaJuan's mom jumped in the conversation, "Go back to your porch Damien before I tell your mom."

Damien said, "Miss Deborah you don't understand. I'm not here to make trouble. I'm here to make peace." He looked at LaJuan and stuck out his hand, "I'm sorry for all the trouble I caused you, and from now on I'm your friend. You can count on me for anything."

LaJuan didn't know what to make of this gesture. Was Damien trying to deceive her with this gesture? She didn't know, but her mom said, "Shake his hand baby. At least he's trying to make up with you."

LaJuan shook his hand, but she was still skeptical. She didn't trust Damien at all. She now had two mysterious things happen to her today.

She said, "Okay Damien." LaJuan then walked away leaving Damien on the sidewalk.

***

LaJuan stared out her mom's bedroom window looking at Damien and his boys. She wondered if he was serious about being friends. Her window was up, and she could hear them talking, but they couldn't see her behind the curtain.

One of the boys said, "We should wait for LaJuan to go to the store or something and whip her behind."

Damien grabbed the boy by the collar and pointed in his face, "Leave LaJuan alone!" He let the boy go and looked over at all the boys, "No one is to touch LaJuan. She's my friend now, and if anyone touches her, they will answer to me. Got it!"

All the boys nodded. LaJuan couldn't believe it. Damien had a change of heart or something. The phone rang, and LaJuan answered it, "Hello."

The voice said, "As you can see we had a talk with Damien and he will not bother you again."

The line went dead. Who were these people? They had her phone number, they talked to Damien and made him leave her alone, but they didn't do anything about her stepdad. Maybe they wanted her to deal with him.

She went back to her room. She made up her mind what she was going to do. If he bothered her tonight, it would be the last night. She said in the mirror, *"One of us will die tonight."*

15

Markus came home from school still on cloud nine. His relationship with Renata was the best thing that had happened to him in his life. Dinner with Renata and her mom was great, and he thoroughly enjoyed every minute of it.

However, now he knew he was going to have to deal with his dad. He didn't tell anyone he would be home late because of dinner. He didn't want his dad to ruin it for him, and he was ready to endure his punishment. However, what he didn't know was that he wasn't going to be the only one punished.

When Markus walked in the house, his mother and sister were in tears. Kyanna had her arms around his mom comforting her while Damien stood watching.

Damien said sternly to Markus, "You caused this." He walked upstairs staring at Markus the entire time.

Kyanna said, "Daddy asked Mommy where you were, and she said she didn't know. Daddy beat her up because she wouldn't tell him. "

Rhonda patted Kyanna on the shoulder, "It's okay baby. I didn't want Markus' date ruined."

"Mom this has got to end. We can't..."

"Come here boy!"

Markus recognized the voice as his father. He turned around, and he was standing by the front door, angry. Markus slowly walked over to him.

"Didn't I tell you to come straight home?"

Markus started to answer but before he could the punch hit him in the stomach and he doubled over, out of breath. Rhonda shouted, "Leave him alone!"

John tried to get to Rhonda, but Markus grabbed his leg and wouldn't let go. John hit him in the face and shoulders trying to free himself. Kyanna shouted, "Stop leave my brother alone!"

Rhonda grabbed Kyanna and ran out the back door. When Markus thought they were safe, he let go of John's leg and curled up in a ball. He felt the belt across his back. It was so hard that a few of the hits ripped his shirt.

Damien shouted, "Dad!" Markus was surprised that Damien even felt bad for him this time.

John stopped and walked out the front door. Markus hoped someone heard the noise and called the police but most of the time the neighbors just mind their own business.

Markus got up, and Damien just stood there looking at him. He had bruises on his face, shoulders, and back. It was the worst beating he endured.

Damien just stared at him. Markus went out the back door looking for his mom and sister. He didn't find them. He hoped they were safe at a neighbor's house. Markus decided to go across the street and sit behind the kindergarten playground area. It was a private spot where he just sat and thought about his life.

He sat there with his head down thinking about how bad his life was. He wondered just how good a life he could have with Renata given what he's going through. Should he tell her about it or not?

He felt a hand touch him on the shoulder and he flinched. It was Andra, "Oh my God Markus what happened?"

"Nothing." Markus stood up and tried to walk away, but Andra wouldn't let it go, "Nothing? You got bruises on your face and your shirt is torn, that's something, Markus."

Markus sharply replied, "It's nothing, just leave it alone okay?"

Andra was in tears. Markus felt bad for snapping at her, but he couldn't discuss the family business.

Andra said, "I'm going to get Renata."

Markus grabbed her, "Please don't. Please!"

Andra looked at Markus, "I need too, someone needs to tell her Markus. You need help."

"She can't give it. No one can help me."

"That's not true, Markus."

"Look, Andra, I'm destined to be in this life. I don't deserve Renata, and if she knew what was happening to me, she would break up with me. Please don't tell her, she doesn't need to be a part of this world."

Andra replied, "Renata wouldn't break up with you because of this. She would help you in any way she could. You should realize how caring she is by now."

"I do know, but I don't want to involve her in this. Please, Andra."

"Okay but you must promise that you will tell her soon."

Markus didn't know if he could promise that but if it would stop Andra from telling Renata then he would promise. He said, "Okay, I promise I will tell her soon."

***

The day came too soon for Markus. He didn't want to go to school for fear that people would see his bruises. Rhonda put some makeup on his face to cover the visible bruises.

Markus didn't want to wear makeup, but it was either that or make up a reason why his face was bruised. He told his mom, "Not too much okay?"

Rhonda said, "People won't even notice."

Markus replied, "We got to get out of here, Mom."

She didn't answer. Markus knew she would never leave. His dad was financially holding them hostage, and he knew it. He had to get a job and help his mother leave that house. That was the only way they would survive.

Damien saw his mother putting makeup on Markus, "What a punk." Markus didn't honor him with a response. He just grabbed his books and headed to school.

Markus got to Renata's house to walk her to the bus stop. He secretly hoped she wasn't going to go to school, but he knew that wouldn't happen.

She came out the door and immediately stared at his face. He knew she could tell. Renata's mom, Allison Smith, walked out the door behind Renata. Renata tried to rub the makeup off his face, but Markus jerked his head away.

She asked, "What happened to you?"

Markus answered, "Nothing, let's just go to school."

Allison wiped the makeup and gasped, "Oh my God. Who did this to you?" She sternly looked at Markus. He already knew that she was not the kind of woman that you lied to or blew off. She demanded an answer.

"I fell...I can be clumsy sometimes. Can we go, Renata?"

Allison grabbed him by the arm, "You didn't fall. Who did this to you?" He looked at her, not wanting to answer. She said, "Never mind. You kids go to school."

Markus was relieved that she let it go and they walked to the bus stop. He hoped that Renata wouldn't bring it up anymore.

On the way to the bus stop, Renata didn't say a word. It made Markus uncomfortable. He wasn't sure if she was going to break up with him or not. He didn't want to ask because he was afraid of the answer.

Andra walked up, "Good morning guys."

Renata quietly and without her usual smile responded, "Morning."

Markus replied, "Good morning, Andra."

She looked at each of them and asked Markus, "She knows?"

Markus didn't answer. He didn't look at Renata either but he could feel her stare. She said sternly, "You told her and not me?"

Andra jumped in, "No he didn't tell me, but he promised he would tell you."

Markus said angrily, "You guys think this is easy? It's not and you won't know it until you've had to live it." He walked off from them. Inside he wanted to cry, but his manhood wouldn't allow it.

Renata walked over and laid her head on his chest. He instinctively put his arm around her and dropped his head on top of hers, "I'm sorry, baby."

Renata looked up at him, "I'm here for you, but you have to let me in." She laid her head back on his chest and the bus drove up. They got on and rode to school mostly in silence.

***

After school, Markus walked Renata back home as usual. When they got to her apartment, her mom was standing on the porch with another woman Markus hadn't seen before.

Allison introduced the woman, "Renata, Markus this is Veda Boykins. Veda this is my daughter Renata and her boyfriend, Markus."

Veda said, "Hi kids how are you?"

Renata answered, "Good."

Markus followed, "Good."

Veda asked, "So Markus where do you live?"

Markus was suspicious. This wasn't the first time that someone tried to have a social worker talk to him. He knew he couldn't allow this because he didn't want to be taken from his mother. Despite everything, he loved his mother, and nothing was going to separate them.

Markus looked away but said, "A few rows down."

Veda asked, "What apartment?"

Markus quickly looked at her, "I have to go." He turned and quickly walked away. He wanted to look back at Renata, but even his love for her wouldn't allow that to happen.

***

Markus hurriedly got back home. When he walked in the door, he found his dad in the living room playing with Kyanna like nothing happened the day before. He saw Markus, "Markus, my son come here."

He hugged Markus, "How was your day son?" Markus couldn't believe he asked that question. Yesterday he beat him and put bruises over his body. Today he's asking him how his day was.

He answered, "It was cool."

John replied, "Good." He patted Markus on the back like he loved his son.

Markus walked into the kitchen where his mom was cooking, "Mom, Renata's mom saw my bruises this morning than when we came home she had a social worker there. She didn't introduce herself as a social worker, but I recognize them when I see them."

Rhonda asked, "What did you tell her?"

Markus said, "Nothing. I know what you said about them breaking us up. I didn't tell her anything."

Rhonda replied anxiously, "You can't tell them, Markus. I know it's not the best here but if they find out they will break us up and I don't have any money to take care of you guys."

Markus wanted to tell the social worker everything, but the look in his mother's eyes wouldn't allow it. He loved her so much and couldn't go against her wishes.

He calmly told his mom, "I won't tell them anything mom, I promise."

Someone knocked at the door, and John answered it. Markus stood there as he argued with whoever was at the door. After a minute Markus realized it was the social worker. His mom looked at him.

Markus said, "I swear I didn't tell her mom."

"I know you didn't son."

John had to let them in the apartment. Veda looked at each of them and then walked over to Rhonda. She stuck out her hand, "Hi my name is Veda Boykins, and I'm here to chat with you and your family."

Rhonda didn't shake her hand, "Why don't you leave us alone?"

Veda replied, "I'm sorry but when there's a complaint filed we have to follow up on it."

John angrily asked, "Complaint? Who filed a complaint?"

"I'm not at liberty to release that information. Now, where is Damien Black?"

Rhonda answered, "He's outside with his friends. I don't know exactly where he's at right now."

Veda looked at Kyanna, "So you must be Kyanna."

Kyanna quickly ran to her dad and hugged him. Markus was disgusted with the hiding they had to do but if they didn't the social worker would split up their home.

Veda asked Rhonda, "I know there's abuse going on here and all of you would be better off if you let me help."

Rhonda said, "We are fine, please leave my family alone."

Veda replied, "Your son has visible bruising on him. Where did that come from?"

Markus answered, "I tripped and fell."

Veda responded, "I know that's not true, Markus."

Markus said, "I don't care what you think you know, but that's what happened."

Rhonda touched Markus, "Be respectful son. My son has answered your question, and you don't have anything to go on so please leave us alone."

Veda said, "I will be filing a report on this case, and my recommendation will be to remove your kids from this home. Now you can make it easy on yourself and tell me the truth."

John said, "Make whatever recommendation you want, without proof and testimony you have nothing."

Veda replied, "You will see me again."

She walked out the house, and Markus was angry. He didn't want to be removed from his family, but he would have loved it if his dad had been removed. He was angry at Renata's mom for sending the social worker to their house. He would have to handle that situation. He hoped it wouldn't come between him and the love of his life.

***

Markus loved Renata, but he was angry with her mom for getting the social worker involved in their family business. For years Markus wanted someone to save them from their horrible life, but his mother refuses to leave because she can't survive without his dad.

The ringing of the phone broke Markus' thoughts. He didn't want to answer fearing it was Renata, but Kyanna did answer it downstairs. She cried out for Damien and Markus was both relieved and sad. Relieved that he didn't have to argue with Renata but sad that it wasn't her that called. He reasoned that she didn't call because of the social worker. Markus told himself he would call her when Damien got off the phone with Brittani.

Markus couldn't understand what Brittani saw in Damien. Every day he was becoming more and more like their dad. Markus feared the worst for his brother and anyone who he dated. He was going to be an abuser that's for sure.

Kyanna walked into the room and smiled at her hero. Despite what the world saw in Markus one person looked up to him, and that was Kyanna. To her, Markus could do no wrong.

"Why do we have to lie to the social worker lady?"

"Because if we tell the truth they will take us from mom. Do you want to live with strangers?"

"Would they beat us like dad?"

"Who knows, it could be worse. I'd rather stay with mom."

Kyanna sat down by him, "Do you think mom will ever leave daddy?"

Markus nodded his head, "No. She believes she can't survive without him. I think we can. It would be hard, and I would have to get a job, but we could do it."

"Why don't you get a job now?"

He was amazed that she asked that question, "Are you serious? He would never let me work. He wouldn't like me making my own money because I would help mom leave."

Kyanna twisted her lips in disgust, "When I get your age I'm going to get a job and leave. I'm going far away, like Sarasota!"

Markus laughed, "Sarasota isn't far Ky. If you want to get away go to Japan or somewhere like that."

"That's far?"

"Yeah like 7,000 miles."

Kyanna's eyes popped opened wide, "Wow...that far? Yeah, I want to go there."

Markus said, "But then you won't see me."

"Oh, well maybe Georgia then."

Markus hugged his little sister, "Yeah, Georgia. Then I can come see you or you can come see me."

"Yeah, that's the ticket."

Rhonda yelled from her bedroom, "Ky are you dressed for bed?"

"No ma'am." She looked at Markus, "Dang."

Markus laughed, and his sister left to get dressed for bed. Markus waited for a while, but Damien tied up the phone. He could hear him talking from the upstairs bedroom.

After a while it got quiet, so Markus went downstairs to see if Damien was still on the phone. He was, and Markus could hear him getting angry with Brittani. He was telling her that she didn't love him because she wouldn't sleep with him.

Markus shook his head in disbelief. His brother was so different from him. Their opinions on the woman were drastically different. Markus hoped Brittani would stick to her beliefs and not give into Damien. That was his brother, but he knew Brittani really meant nothing to Damien.

Damien slammed the phone down and cursed. Markus walked the rest of the way down the stairs and asked, "You done with the phone."

Damien didn't respond he went upstairs and Markus dialed Renata's number. Her mom answered, "Hello." Markus thought, *"Dang, why did she have to answer?"* He said, "Hi Miss Smith, may I speak to Renata?"

She answered, "Renata's asleep right now. She went to bed early."

Markus sighed but not loud enough for her to hear, "Okay, would you tell her I called?"

"Sure. Take care Markus."

"I will, thank you, Miss Smith. Goodnight."

"Goodnight baby."

Markus was disappointed. He didn't want to talk to her about the social worker, but he did want to hear her voice.

16

Damien was standing outside watching all of the kids go off to school. He had argued with Brittani before she got on the bus. He felt their relationship was about over because she wouldn't have sex with him.

LaJuan was on her way to the store. Damien ran over. He looked at her, and she looked at him. He decided to break the ice, "Hey LaJuan, how are you?"

She looked puzzled, "Hi, Damien."

Damien said, "You look nice today."

LaJuan turned her head, "Okay, what the Hell is going on here? Why are you trying to be so nice to me now? We both know the deal."

"LaJuan, I am serious. All the stuff I did to you in the past is in the past. I want to be your friend from now on. Really?"

LaJuan stared at him. Her stare was so hard that Damien thought she was staring through him. He continued, "Where you headed?"

LaJuan answered, "To the store. We don't have any milk for cereal."

A car slowly pulled to a stop on 22nd Street near the two kids. The window rolled down, and the lady said, "Hi Damien. Can I talk to you for a minute?"

Damien firmly replied, "No. I know who you are. Leave me and my family alone!"

She got out the car. Damien pointed his finger and shouted, "Leave me alone lady!"

Veda stopped in her tracks. LaJuan didn't know what was going on, but she chimed in, "Leave my friend alone. He clearly doesn't want to talk to you."

Damien looked at LaJuan. He had gotten through to her, and they were friends after so many years of fighting they were now friends.

Veda got back into her car and drove off. Damien looked at LaJuan, "Hey thanks. You stood up for me. I appreciate that."

LaJuan poked him in the chest, "You better not be playing with me."

"I'm not. I really want to be your friend LaJuan. I even told my friends to leave you alone from now on. You'll see things are going to be different between us."

LaJuan smiled. She hadn't done that in a long time. It actually felt weird on her face. She lightly punched Damien in the shoulder, "So, what's on your agenda for this suspended day?"

Damien laughed, "I have no idea. It's been so boring."

"Well, I guess we can hang out. Boring won't be so bad when it's two of us. Besides, I need somewhere to be, so I don't have to deal with my stepdad."

"Is it that bad? You know he's friends with my dad right?"

"Yes I do, and I can't stand either of them. Sorry, but your dad is just as bad as my stepdad."

Damien didn't respond. He didn't like negative talk about his dad. He decided to change the conversation.

"I think Brittani is going to break up with me."

LaJuan quickly looked at him, "Really...why?"

Damien smirked, "Well, it's kinda like..."

"She won't have sex with you, right?"

Damien stopped in his tracks, "How'd you know that?"

"Come on Damien who in all of Adams Junior High doesn't know that you're trying your best to get in her pants?"

"Wow, I didn't know everyone knew."

"We do, but you need to realize, we are only 14 years old and shouldn't be having sex."

Damien looked down, "Everyone has but me."

LaJuan laughed, "Please don't tell me you believe all your friends? Trust me, they lying. Look at the statistics man, only 1 in 5 females has sex before the age of 15. Brittani is a good girl, and you would do well to ease up and stop pressing her for sex. In the long run, it could work out for you."

"You think so?" "Yeah, I do." "Wow, I'm taking advice from LaJuan Craig...who would have thunk it?"

They both laughed and continued their walk to the store. Damien had a friend, and it was someone he didn't expect to be his friend. He didn't know why the men in suits wanted him to be friends with her but learned that she was a really cool person.

17

Markus practically ran to Renata's house the next day. He was nervous that she might not want to be with him now. The social worker lady messed up everything.

He got to her apartment and knocked on the back door. Her mom answered, "Hi Markus, she's on her way down. Have a seat."

Markus sat down. He tried not to appear anxious, but he couldn't help it. Renata came bopping down the stairs, happy as ever. When she hit the bottom, she started dancing. Markus couldn't do anything but laugh. She wasn't mad at him.

Markus stood up and hugged his girl, "Good morning."

She replied, "Good morning sweetie." She let her arms lay on his shoulders, turned her head and smiled seductively at Markus. He was paralyzed with love.

She asked, "Are you going to kiss me good morning?"

Markus was shocked. He hadn't kissed her in the mouth before, and her mom was standing in the kitchen. He didn't want to get killed. He said, "But, your mom?"

"She's not looking."

He kissed her lightly on the lips.

"I saw that!"

Renata quickly picked up her purse, "Bye mom!" She grabbed Markus by the hand and led him out the door.

Markus was more than happy to follow. He would follow her to the ends of the Earth and back, but at this moment he wanted to get away from Allison before she killed them both.

***

School was going rather uneventful for Markus. He was one of the smartest kids in the school but because he was from the projects he didn't get put in classes that were challenging to him. Many of the school's teachers felt he should be going to a private school that could accelerate his learning but his parents couldn't afford it.

Markus was sitting in the last period of the day when a student came in the room. Everyone knew someone was getting called to the office when this particular student came in the room with the blue tickets.

Markus was never called to the office. He never got in trouble, so he wasn't paying attention when the teacher called his name the first time.

One of his classmates tapped him on the arm to get his attention. The teacher was standing there obviously feeling put off by Markus' lack of attention.

Markus got up, took the blue ticket and headed to the office. He had no idea what the front office could want with him.

The path to the office would take him by Andra's class, so he wanted to look inside and wave at his friend. He believed Paula was in that class also.

He got to their classroom, and the door was open. He walked pass and saw the teacher's head was down and she was writing. He looked at Andra and Paula. They waved at him, and he made them laugh. They were great people and made him feel like he mattered. He wasn't comfortable around a lot of kids but those two he was good with them.

He pressed on to the front office. He went into the office and was told to have a seat. A few minutes later the dean came out and asked him to come into his office. Mr. Davis was a science teacher last year who got promoted to dean. Most kids felt he was mean and strict. His daughters were off limits to anyone. Markus didn't mind that part because they were much younger than him.

Along the walls were pictures of his family. He recognized Mr. Davis' wife Mrs. Davis from his time at Adams Junior High. Markus liked her very much. While he was there, she stopped people from picking on him. One day Markus met Penny Davis, Mr. Davis' oldest daughter. Markus thought she was mature and very polite. One day she was going to make a great wife like her mother.

A big painting of Mrs. Davis, Penny, Nya and Raine sat on the wall behind Mr. Davis' chair. He knew Mr. Davis was proud of that painting.

Mr. Davis sat up in the chair ready to talk but was interrupted, "Daddy, can I have this candy bar?"

Markus looked and recognized Mr. Davis' youngest daughter, Raine. She was a pretty little girl. Markus smiled at her, and she smiled back. Raine reminded Markus of his little sister.

Mr. Davis said, "Okay, but don't tell your mom."

He smiled, and Raine said, "Thank you!" She ran off, and Mr. Davis' face shifted back to business. Markus didn't know what he had done, but the look on Mr. Davis' face wasn't making him feel good.

Mr. Davis began, "Markus, you're a fine student here, and my wife tells me you were an outstanding student at Adams. Both of us are concerned about your home life."

Markus had the feeling in his stomach again. Mrs. Davis tried to get him to talk about his home life two years ago, and now Mr. Davis is trying to do the same. *"Why can't they just leave us alone?"*

Mr. Davis continued, "Son if you're having difficulty at home, we can help you. We can get the right people involved to help you get through your problems. You don't have to suffer alone."

Markus shuffled in his seat. *"What did he know about it? His life is perfect. Look at his family, not an issue there!"* He didn't know what to say so he chose not to say anything and pray that the bell would ring. He didn't believe God cared one bit about him, but he hoped this time God would help him out of this conversation.

Markus just looked in Mr. Davis' eyes. Mr. Davis asked him, "Do you want us to help you son?"

Markus managed to say with his head down, "No sir. We don't have any issues. I'm fine."

He wondered how and why all of a sudden Mr. Davis got involved. Did

Renata tell him? Did her mom call the school? Did the social worker report it? He didn't know.

Mr. Davis said, "Son there is nothing we can do for you if you don't tell us what's going on. Your teachers noticed the bruising on your face. Your PE teacher also noticed bruising on your back. Let us help you."

"Dang makeup didn't cover anything!" Markus shuffled around in his seat some more, "I just fell down the stairs in our apartment. It was a nasty fall. I'll be okay."

At least he knew Renata hadn't dimed him out. He wouldn't know how to take that if she did turn his family in like her mom did.

Mr. Davis patted his hands on his big desk and looked at the clock. School was about to end, and Markus couldn't have been happier. Mr. Davis stood up and extended his hand to Markus.

Markus stood up and shook his hand, "If there's anything I can do for you Markus, please let me know. I wanna help you."

Markus answered him, "Yes sir, I'll remember that sir."

Mr. Davis said, "You can go back to class."

Markus couldn't have moved any faster. He wanted out of that office as quick as he could. He wanted to tell him all about his good for nothing father, but he couldn't risk hurting his mom.

***

Markus and Renata reached her front door. They could hear Renata's mom in the house singing. Renata turned to Markus and asked, "Do you want to pray with me?"

Markus was stunned. He didn't even know how to pray. He answered, "I don't know how." He was embarrassed but once again she calmed him, "No worries, I'll show you. Come in."

They went into the house, and Allison greeted them, "Hi kids. How was your day?" Markus wasn't use to so much happiness. If his dad was home, there would barely be a greeting from anyone because the atmosphere was so tensed.

Renata answered, "My day was blessed momma, how about yours?"

"Oh, I had a great day! I got a new job, and I start Monday. Praise the Lord!"

"Yes! Praise the Lord."

Markus said, "Congratulations Miss Smith. That's great."

Renata said, "Momma, Markus wants to pray with me."

"Really, well I'll go upstairs and let you two have the living room. No kissing young lady."

Renata covered her mouth in embarrassment, "Yes ma'am."

Allison walked upstairs and Renata led Markus to the couch where they kneeled down.

Markus heard people pray in church but he had never done it himself. He didn't know what to say but Renata took over for him.

She said, "Praying is just having a conversation with God. First, let's look at the Bible." She pulled the Bible from the coffee table and opened it. "Okay in Matthew chapter six Jesus tells us how to pray."

"He says, 'And when you pray, you shall not be like the hypocrites. For they love to pray standing in the synagogues and on the corners of the streets, that they may be seen by men. Assuredly, I say to you, they have their reward. But you, when you pray, go into your room, and when you have shut your door, pray to your Father who is in the secret place; and your Father who sees in secret will reward you openly. And when you pray, do not use vain repetitions as the heathen do. For they think that they will be heard for their many words.'

'Therefore do not be like them. For your Father knows the things you have need of before you ask Him. In this manner, therefore, pray:'

'Our Father in heaven, Hallowed be Your name. Your kingdom come.
Your will be done on earth as it is in heaven. Give us this day our daily bread. And forgive us our debts, as we forgive our debtors. And do not lead us into temptation, but deliver us from the evil one. For Yours is the kingdom and the power and the glory forever. Amen.'"

She closed the book and looked at Markus, "That is how you pray. Are you ready?"

Markus was nervous, "Yeah."

Renata took his hand, "I'll do it today and you practice at home tonight. Let's bow our heads."

"Father we come before you today thanking you for the very breath of life itself. There are many who have been called home but we are not one of them. Instead we are here to continue your kingdom work."

"Father thank you for this wonderful man who is my boyfriend. He doesn't know you like I do but Father give me the words to show him your way. Let me and my family be a guide to help him through his troubles. Let me show him that you have not forsaken him or his family."

"On this day Father we bind the enemy. We ask that nothing penetrate my friend's spirit, let him know true happiness. Let him know the happiness that comes from a life of serving you God. Surround him with your angels and let no one harm him."

Father...I ask this in your wonderful and matchless son's name, Jesus Christ. Amen."

Markus raise his head and looked deeply into Renata's eyes. She was smiling. She had that glow that he had come to enjoy. He leaned over to kiss her, "Oh no you don't!"

He quickly jumped back when he heard Allison, "I told y'all no kissing and I meant that."

"Momma you were listening?"

"You doggone right! Nice prayer baby."

"Thank you momma. I learned from the best."

Allison put her arm around Markus, "Son, we're here for you. I'm sorry about inviting Veda over to talk to you. In hindsight that was probably too much too fast. But anytime you need to get away from your house you can come here. As long as I'm home you can come. You are not to be alone with my daughter. I like you but not that much!"

They all laughed and Markus felt a peace that he had never felt before.

18

Markus returned to his apartment and nearly fainted when he saw Damien sitting next to LaJuan and they were laughing and talking.

"What's going on here?"

"Hi Markus, I was wrong about your brother. He's pretty cool after all."

"My brother, Damien, is cool?"

Damien stood up like he was going to fight his brother, "What you trying to say punk?" He turned to LaJuan, "You just don't know how much of a punk this guy is LaJuan."

"Damien stop being mean. That's your brother."

"Yeah that's not my fault."

LaJuan laughed and pushed Damien slightly, "You silly. Markus don't pay that any attention. You cool...and fine."

Damien snapped, "What? Tell me you kidding? He ain't got nothing on me!"

LaJuan laughed and Markus went into the house. He couldn't believe the kind of person his little brother had turned into. He was arrogant, rude and mean but somehow he had convinced LaJuan to like him.

Inside Kyanna came running to her big brother. She was always happy to see him, especially when their dad wasn't home. This was the case this time. Kyanna excitedly said, "Daddy's in jail!"

"What? Why?"

"Momma said he got into a fight at a bar this morning and they took him to jail. She's trying to get money to get him out. I hope she doesn't get it."

"Me either. Where's momma?"

"Upstairs. Oh and your food is in the oven."

"Thanks Ky." Markus went into the kitchen to get his food. The phone rang and he assumed his mother answered it upstairs. She called down, "Ky is Markus home?"

Kyanna answered, "Yes ma'am."

"Tell him to pick up the phone."

Markus picked up the phone, "Got it. Hello."

Renata answered, "Hey bae, do you want to go to Bible study tonight with me and my mom?"

Markus didn't like the church stuff but he loved Renata, and it was another chance to spend time with her, so he was excited at the chance. "I'll have to ask my mom."

"Okay, I'll hold."

Markus sat the phone down and ran upstairs, "Mom, Renata wants me to go to Bible study with them tonight. Can I go?"

"I need you to stay with your brother and sister. I'm going to see if I can bail your dad out."

"Why? You should let him rot."

"That's my husband Markus and your father. Don't talk like that. Tell Renata maybe next week okay?"

Markus didn't like that. He turned and went back downstairs to the phone, "I can't go because she needs me to watch my brother and sister."

"Oh, I'm sorry. I will pray for you all tonight, okay?"

"Okay. I really wish I could go with you."

"I wish you could too but don't be late picking me up tomorrow Mr. Black."

"I won't, ever."

She laughed, "Okay, goodnight sweetie."

"Goodnight honey."

***

Markus helped Kyanna with her homework and then played board games with her until it was bedtime. Every chance he got, he thought about Renata and wondered how Bible study was going. Something inside of him was changing, but he couldn't understand what it was. Was it his feelings for Renata or was it something else?

She was great and knew he loved her, but something else was different since she prayed for him. He couldn't wait for Kyanna's bedtime so he could pray again. It would be his first time, but he was excited about it.

The time for Kyanna to go to bed had come, and she kissed her big brother on the jaw. She thumbed her nose up at Damien and went to sleep.

Markus didn't care about Damien he was old enough to be on his own and Damien wouldn't listen to him anyway.

Markus went into the bedroom and knelt down at his bed. He didn't know what to say, but he remembered Renata saying to just have a conversation with God.

He put his hands together and closed his eyes, "God, this house does not know peace. We live under the dark weight of the fear every day. I'm not sure what I'm doing, but I pray for your protection and for help and understanding from my friends. I pray for strength for my mom. Give her the power to leave this house before it is too late. God help my father. Help him to understand the pain he's causing. We are his children, and my mom is his wife. Help him to know that we love him and want him to stop abusing us. Make my home a happy, Christian home. God protect my baby sister. She is so innocent and deserves better. Help me to keep her safe. I don't know what else to say God but help us! Amen."

He got up and got in his bed. He felt better after praying and slowly drifted off to sleep with thoughts of his favorite girl, Renata.

***

Markus wasn't sure what time it was when the yelling woke him up, but he was greatly concerned for his mother. He ran to her room, but the door was closed and locked. He could hear his heartless father beating her, forcing her to have sex with him.

He shouted, "Momma!"

Rhonda answered, "It's okay baby, go back to bed."

Markus sat on the floor and cried. He said under his breath, "I guess God doesn't love me either."

19

After Bible study, Renata was sitting on her bed thinking about her life and Markus. She knew some idea of what he was going through at home. Anyone who looked close enough could see the scars. They can see the pain in his eyes, but he won't let anyone help.

She couldn't understand why he'd rather suffer in silence than to tell her or get help from Miss Boykins. One thing she knew for sure was that she wasn't going to give up. She was going to find a way to get help for Markus, but the first thing she had to do was get him in church.

Allison walked into the room and hugged Renata, "Baby that was nice of you to ask everyone to pray for Markus and his family."

"Thanks, momma. Why do people not want to help? You would think that if he's suffering like I think he is that would make him jump at the chance to get help."

Allison sat down and put her arm around Renata, "Baby, when I was a child my aunt suffered in silence. She didn't want to leave because she felt she couldn't survive on her own, she thought Uncle Elmore would change, and she even blamed herself for the abuse. Honey, she told me once after it was over that she often felt trapped. I believe Markus' mom is feeling the same way."

"What can I do to help him?"

"You're already doing it, baby. Teaching him to pray was a great move and asking everyone at church to pray for him was great also. Now invite him to church Sunday. If you keep introducing him to Jesus, he will be saved."

"Thanks, Momma."

"You love this boy don't you?"

"I don't know. I like him a lot but I don't know what love is yet?"

Allison smiled, "When you wake up in the morning who do you think about?"

"Markus."

"How about before you go to sleep?"

Renata smiled and her head went back, "Markus."

Allison got up and slowly walked out the room, smiling at her daughter as she left. Renata knew in her heart that she loved Markus and her mom just made it clear. She loved her
mom. She was always there for her with advice, love and sometimes a good scolding. That made Renata chuckle.

She rolled back the covers and sheets to her bed and curled up in it. She laughed as she thought of Markus and slowly fell off to sleep.

***

Renata woke up the next morning happy and alert. She chuckled again as she realized her mom was right. The first person she thought of was Markus. She often got up early to take her time to get dressed and listen to music.

After getting dressed, she ran downstairs and kissed her mom on the cheek, "Morning, Momma!"

"Good morning, baby. How'd you sleep?"

"Great and you?"

"Well, I slept very well until I got a call from your dad early this morning."

"Really, what did he want?"

Allison turned to Renata, "He wants you to come up to New York for Christmas."

The look of concern was clearly on Allison's face. Renata just stared. She hadn't seen her father in years, but she loved her mother and didn't want to spend Christmas in New York. Not to mention away from her first boyfriend on their first Christmas.

Renata said, "Well, Momma, we haven't been apart for Christmas...well ever, and I don't want to start this year. I love daddy, but I don't want to go."

Allison replied, "He's your father, and he deserves a chance to see you, baby."

"But I don't want to go."

"Is it that you don't want to be apart from me or Markus?"

Renata smiled, "Both."

"Okay sweetheart, I'll talk to him again and let him know his baby girl is in love."

The smile on Renata face lit up the room. She was in love, and she couldn't believe it. She knew she liked Markus when they started talking, but she didn't know she would fall in love so quickly. She liked the feeling of being in love. She looked out the window and saw Markus coming to the back door. Her heart skipped a beat.

20

Markus was standing at Renata's back
door. Before he could knock the door
flung open, and she stepped out and
embraced him. Allison said, "I know y'all
kissing out there!"

Renata answered, "No, Momma." She
smiled and invited Markus in the house.

It always made him feel good to come in
the Smith's home. No matter what
occurred at his house, their house always
eased the pain.

Renata was bouncier than ever. Markus
wondered what was making her so happy
this morning. He said, "Hi, Miss Smith."

"Good morning Markus, how are you
doing?"

Markus just shrugged his shoulders,
"Okay."

Allison replied, "If you need to talk, I'm
here Markus."

"Thanks, Miss Smith."

Renata took his hand and smiled, "Let's go, sweetie."

That always cheered Markus up. Whenever she uttered the word 'sweetie' it did something inside of him. He led her out the front door and toward the bus stop.

Markus decided to open up to Renata a bit, "Last night I prayed."

She quickly looked at him with a smile, "What? That's wonderful Markus! I'm so happy for you."

"Well, it didn't go so well. I don't think God loves me at all."

"Markus why would you say something like that?"

Markus pitifully looked at her, "Because later that night my mom...she...was screaming. He was abusing her again." Tears began to well up in his eyes. He was trying his best to suppress them, "I tried to help her and all she said was, 'It's okay.' I can't believe she lets him do her like that and where was God? I prayed and everything!"

Renata stopped, and Markus feared he had said something wrong. He put his arm around her and whispered, "Help me, help me to understand, Renata." A tear rolled down his face, and she wiped it away. He felt love at the same time he felt pain. All the times he had suffered during and after a violent episode at home were different than this one. This time he had someone to talk to, someone he loved.

Renata said, "I will help you, Markus. I'm always here for you. God does love you, but he doesn't move in our time. He moves in his time, and we have to be patient sometimes. Sometimes our blessings will come in minutes, most of the time they take longer. It's working out in your favor, trust me. If not me, then trust Him. I do."

Markus kicked some trash on the ground, "If you do, then so do I."

They hugged, and Markus felt better. He wanted to tell her that he loved her but he was afraid. If he said that she might feel overwhelmed and back off. He didn't want that.

Renata softly kissed him on the lips, "I love you, Markus."

He thought he was going to have a heart attack. She said it first and suddenly all the pain of the night before wasn't there anymore. He excitedly replied, "I love you, too."

She smiled and turned to walk away, "I said it first."

He quickly caught up, "But I said it with more feeling!"

"Please dude, give it a rest. I said it first, and you can never change that." She laughed, and Markus put his arm around Renata. She was his girl, and no one could change that now. He was truly in love with the girl of his dreams and even better she loved him back.

***

Markus couldn't wait for the bell to ring for lunch. He had a date with the girl of his dreams. He kept watching the clock, and it seemed to take five minutes to move one minute. He knew that was his imagination, but it seemed that way.

Finally, it rang, and he quickly got up and walked out the class. He almost ran over Andra in the hallway. Andra laughed, "Dude, where's the fire!"

Markus laughed, "I'm on my way to have lunch with the prettiest girl in the world."

Andra said, "Oh my goodness. You two are sick, but I'm happy for you."

Markus smiled. He knew she genuinely was happy for him, "Thanks, Andra. You're the best."

"Yeah I know, now hurry along to your date." She laughed and walked to her next class.

Markus got the lunchroom. Renata is talking to the one person in the school that Markus hated. Paul Hunter was the star of the football team and a bully. They never liked each other.

Markus decided to go up to them. He marveled at his confidence. A couple of weeks ago he would have walked away with his head down.

He got in earshot of the conversation and heard Renata saying, "I don't care what you or anyone else thinks. I love Markus Black and nobody on God's green Earth will change that. If I can't bring Markus, then I won't be there either." She handed him a piece of paper that Markus assumed was an invitation. Paul didn't say anything. He took the paper and walked away.

Markus smiled and walked up behind Renata, "Hey baby."

"Hey!" She hugged him and kissed him.

Markus was on top of the world, "So what did he invite you too?"

"Oh, you heard that?"

"Just the end of it."

"He invited me to his party and had the nerve to tell me to come alone. I told him if my boyfriend can't come then I'm not going. Who the heck invites you to a party where you can't bring your boyfriend?"

"Probably because I'm your boyfriend. Paul always bullies me so, of course, he wouldn't want me at his party."

Renata said, "Well he won't have me there either." The two laughed and enjoy their lunch together.

Markus didn't want it to end. Each time he looked at her was better than the last time. He never wanted them to end.

***

The school day ended, and Markus walked Renata home. He wanted to stay a little longer, but he knew what the price was for doing that. When he got home, no one appeared to be home, so he had to use his key to get in. That was rare because his mom didn't work and was always home.

He ran upstairs to use the bathroom but heard a noise coming from his room. He opened the door and found Damien and LaJuan in the bed together. He quickly closed the door in shock.

Damien burst out the door, "Please don't tell."

LaJuan came out after him, looked at Markus in shame, and ran down the stairs and out the front door.

"Damien, I can't believe you."

"Why because I lost my virginity and you still haven't. It's not my fault you're some kind of love sick sissy. That girl you're with gave it up to a lot of dudes, and now she's singing the Christian stuff to you. You punking out."

Markus got angry and pinned Damien against the wall, "You listen to me you little punk, Renata is a good clean Christian woman who hasn't had sex with anyone. You better respect my girlfriend, or it will be me and you fighting. Trust me, you don't want that."

Markus couldn't believe himself. He had changed. Renata had changed him. He was out of his shell, filled with confidence and not afraid to stand up for his girl.

Damien was smiling, "Well look who grew some balls."

Markus let Damien go, "I mean it." He walked into the bathroom and stared in the mirror.

For the first time in his life, he wasn't a victim. The next step was to convince his mother to stop being a victim. He didn't know how he was going to do it, but somehow he had to do it.

21

LaJuan was lying in her bed, smiling and happy. She couldn't believe what she did with Damien earlier. It was nothing like the horrible experiences she had in the past. With Damien, she wanted to do it, and he made her feel special. Something she hadn't felt in her life.

But now it was the worst part of the day, and she was home in her room. But this time she was prepared. She was not going to be the victim anymore. She looked under her mattress to see if the knife was there. It was, and that was reassuring. If he tried something tonight, she would defend herself, and she didn't care what the consequences were.

She had music playing in the background. It was calming and made her feel good. She loved to listen to contemporary jazz. Among her peers, she was strange like that. Most of the people her age didn't listen to jazz at all but she loved it.

She drifted off to sleep until suddenly she was awakened. He was in the room, rubbing her thigh. The moment had come, but she froze. She found herself wishing Damien was there to help. Could she do it?

He lifted her nightgown up and pulled her panties down. He climbed on top of her and whispered in her ear, "I missed you so much."

She knew he didn't notice her reaching under her mattress. She got the knife firmly into the palm of her hand held it tightly. She visualized thrusting it into him.

She prepared herself and waited until he was so into what he was doing that he never noticed her raising the knife. She quickly plunged it into his side, perforating his heart.

Blood gushed everywhere, and he screamed loud. She pushed his limp body off of her, and she screamed.

Her mom burst through the door and screamed, "What have you done? LaJuan, what have you done?"

LaJuan just stood there. Inside she wanted to smile. She was glad he was dead. He would never rape her again. She was angered by her mother. She was trying her best to revive him. She knew what he did to her, but she still wanted him alive.

Suddenly, her mother rose up and struck her with the back of her hand, knocking LaJuan to the ground. Blood dripped from LaJuan's lip.

LaJuan was angry. *"How could she side with him? This man raped me repeatedly for three years, and she's crying over him!"*

Her mother picked up the knife. LaJuan heard sirens outside. The police were coming. She went into her mother's bedroom and got the revolver out of the drawer. She came back in the room and looked at her mom.

Anger filled her heart. Her mom was crying over the death of a rapist, a rapist who repeatedly raped her only child. Then she had the nerve to slap her to the ground. She had to pay too.

She raised the gun and aimed it at her mother, "Momma."

Deborah turned around and slowly stood up, "What are you doing? You're in enough trouble, young lady. Put that gun..."

She pulled the trigger three times hitting her mom in the chest each time. LaJuan was a natural. She had imagined killing them both so many times that she knew exactly what to do.

She sat down on the floor and waited for the police. She smiled and realized that she would never be abused again.

22

Damien was outside with everyone else wondering what exactly went on next door. He heard the shots and everyone was whispering their opinions.

The ambulance wheeled out two bodies and Damien prayed it wasn't LaJuan. He never prayed before, but he found himself quietly praying. After the bodies were out of the apartment, LaJuan came out with two female police officers. They had her in handcuffs.

Damien knew she had killed her parents. As LaJuan walked by she blew a kiss at Damien and uttered the words, "I'm free."

Damien said, "Yes you are."

He followed her as they took her to the police car waiting on the street. When they were pulling off LaJuan waved bye to Damien.

Part of him was relieved that she wouldn't be raped by her stepdad anymore. She told him earlier what was happening to her and he encouraged her to take action. Somehow he reasoned that all of this had to do with the men in suits. Somehow he knew they would help LaJuan.

Rhonda came up to Damien and put her arm around him, "I know you and LaJuan became friends honey and I'm sorry she's going to jail."

Damien replied, "I'm not. She should have killed them."

Rhonda was shocked, "Damien...you can't condone murder."

"Oh and what about her stepdad who was raping her all the time? He got what he deserved."

"Damien you don't know what was really happening in that house."

Damien looked coldly at his mother. He was growing more impatient with her every day. He felt his dad was right and she was worthless. He walked away in disgust.

His dad was waiting for him at the front door, "Come on in son. I know you're feeling for your friend, but you have to be emotionless. You can't let what happen to others get you down."

"Dad, they got what they deserve for what they were doing to LaJuan."

"I don't doubt that son. She has my respect."

Damien felt his dad truly understood and was right about everything. You have to stand your ground, defend yourself and if necessary kill the person who was hurting you. *"Mom doesn't get it, and that's why she's always getting her butt kicked."*

Damien went upstairs and got into his bed. Everyone else was still outside. He thought about LaJuan and hoped she would be alright, but he now understood that in this world you have to be the tough one. The one to stand up, take what you want and press on. LaJuan refused to be abused, and he admired her for what she did. He wondered if he could kill someone if he needed to do it.

***

It was early the next morning before the junior high school kids left for school. John went to work, Rhonda took Kyanna to school because she missed the bus and Markus left early to meet Renata.

Damien answered the front door. It was Brittani, and he invited her inside. He thought Brittani was beautiful as usual and she made him forget all about LaJuan.

Brittani asked, "What happened last night? I heard LaJuan killed her parents."

Damien answered, "Yeah that's what it looks like."

"Wow, I can't believe she did that."

"Why not? He was raping her, and she let it happen. They both deserved it."

Brittani was staring at him. Damien continued, "Oh you didn't know that?"

Brittani answered, "No, she never said anything like that. I mean, we weren't girls or nothing but nobody I knew, knew that about her at all."

"LaJuan is tough, and that's the way you should be. Never let anyone push you around. Take what you want and never be anybody's victim. My dad said he's right."

Brittani said, "No Damien, your dad is wrong. Love thy neighbor not kill thy neighbor."

Damien didn't even realize that he slapped her until she fell to the ground, "Don't you use that Bible stuff to mock my dad!" He grabbed her by the throat and put his face in hers, "Don't make me put you in your place!"

Markus shouted from behind, "Damien, let her go!"

Damien let her go and turned to his brother, "What you gonna do? I'll take you out just like LaJuan took her miserable parents out."

Markus looked at Brittani. She was scared. He said, "Brittani go home."

Damien blocked her way, "I didn't say she could leave. I'm in control here, not you."

Markus sternly said, "Move Damien and let her leave."

Rhonda walked in the front door, and Damien moved. Brittani ran out the door.

Rhonda asked, "What's going on here?"

Damien pushed passed her and went upstairs. He slammed the door to his room and paced the floor. He thought, *"Dad would've beaten both of them. Hell, LaJuan would have taken them both out but me...I couldn't do anything. I've got to do better. Markus your day is coming. I'm going to put you in your place. Then dad and LaJuan will love and respect me!"*

23

Markus' heart was truly saddened by his brother's actions. He knew he was gone completely to his dad's opinion, but now with the LaJuan incident, he was totally gone. He wondered what Damien would have done to Brittani if he hadn't walked in the house. He was afraid for Brittani and would make it a point to go see her after school. He wanted her to know that not all the Blacks were bad people.

He got back to Renata's house, and she met him outside, "Hey dude, what took you so long?"

"There was an incident with Damien. I caught him about to beat up his girlfriend."

Renata's mouth dropped, "What? Are you serious?"

"Yeah, he's turning out to be just like our father."

Renata nodded, "Oh my God. That poor girl."

"Yeah, I'm going to go over and talk to her after school. Will you go with me?"

Renata pepped up, "Yeah, heck yeah, let's do it. We're a team, and we can change the world, sweetie."

Markus realized that she was joking, but she did have a great idea about changing the world. He wanted to start an organization that would fight against abuse. Maybe he could start it with the love of his life?

"Yes, we can, sweetheart and it all starts now."

Renata smiled, and they walked hand-in-hand to the bus stop.

***

School was over, and the bus let everyone out at the usual 22nd Street bus stop. Markus and Renata headed to Brittani's house. Markus lived five rows farther away from the bus stop than Renata and Brittani lived in between. So Renata dropped her books off at home and then they headed to Brittani's.

When they got there, Brittani was standing on the porch with two of her girlfriends. She appeared to still be shaken.

, "Hi, Brittani," Markus said.

"Hi," She replied.

"I just came to apologize for this morning. My brother is way off the deep end."

Brittani said, "I'm scared of him."

Renata put her arm around Brittani, "I can understand how you feel. Don't go around him anymore."

Brittani said, "Trust me, I won't."

Markus replied, "We all aren't like Damien, Brittani and I'm going to do what I can to help my brother even if it means confronting my dad."

Brittani said, "Don't make it bad for yourself, Markus. I'll be okay. I will just stay away from him."

"As his brother, I can't stay away, and I can't turn a blind eye. I need to help him."

Renata said, "'We' sweetie, we need to help him. We're a team."

Markus smiled, "Yes, 'we' need to help him."

Brittani smiled, "You're a nice guy Markus, and you guys make a good Christian couple. I like it. I hope I find someone like you, Markus."

Renata said, "Awwww...that's so sweet. Thank you!"

No one had ever referred to Markus as a Christian. Although he had been to church a lot, he was never baptized. He didn't want to say he wasn't a Christian because he did believe in Jesus Christ but he didn't feel he was even worthy of being called that.

Markus replied, "Yeah thanks, Brittani. Well, we better go, honey."

"Okay, bye guys!"

Everyone said 'bye,' and Markus and Renata strolled off.

Markus asked Renata, "What does it take to be a Christian? Do you just have to be baptized or is there more to it?"

Renata smiled, "Well, being baptized is the washing away of the sin after you have accepted Jesus Christ. I forget where it is in the Bible, but as long as you believe that Jesus is the Son of God, that He is your Lord and Savior and that He died for your sins, then you are a Christian. After that, you get baptized."

"I see. I've been going to church for a while but I never really thought about it. Given how my family is, I just thought church was something everyone went to, pretended to be happy and love the Lord then went home to all the mess you left."

"Wow, really? That's not how it should be Markus. As Christians, we aren't perfect, but we try to live right. Come to church with me on Sunday. You'll enjoy it."

"I will."

"Sweet, well get home before you have to deal with more drama."

"Thanks, baby, I love you!"

She laughed, "I love you, too."

"I beat you that time."

Renata waved her finger back and forth, "Doesn't matter I was first period. You can never beat that."

"Okay." Markus ran home, happy and excited. Would he ever have a time when he left Renata's house not happy? He didn't think he would. He did dread going back home. His father would probably have more drama, and his mother would take a beating just to keep his paycheck in the house. He didn't like it, but he couldn't change it.

When Markus got home, his father and Damien were talking. His father pushed Damien out the way confronted Markus.

"You were fighting your brother?"

Markus said, "We argue, but we didn't..."

John punched Markus in the chest. Markus fell to one knee. The pain throbbed through his body. John then slapped him across his face, "If I find out you're fighting your brother again, it'll be worse than this for you."

Markus looked up, and Damien was smirking. He grabbed his books and walked out the door.

John yelled, "Get your behind here!"

Markus dropped the books and ran. He ran as fast as he could. He didn't stop until he arrived at Young Junior High school. He figured no one was there and he would be alone.

He sat on the floor by the front office and cried. He hadn't cried in a long time, but today he did. Every time he had happiness it was taken away from him. The demon would rise its head up and steal his joy.

"Are you okay?"

Markus didn't recognize the voice. He didn't want to look up either. He was ashamed of his tears.

"It's okay to cry. My mom says a good cry cleans the soul."

He smiled and looked up, "Hey I remember you from the dean's office."

"Yeah, he's my dad. I go there every day after school to ride home with him. My name is Raine...Raine Davis. What's your name?"

"Markus Black. Thanks for your kind words. How old are you?"

"Six...do you go to church?"

"Well, I'm going Sunday to my girlfriend's church. It's Saint Matthews on Lake."

Raine smiled, "Really, that's where I go. I'm singing a song, so you'll get to hear me sing."

Markus said, "You are? You can sing that well?"

"Yeah, we all can sing. Me and my sisters have been singing since we were born. Our whole family is into music."

Markus stood up. This little girl made him feel better, "That's great. I will be there to check you out."

"Okay. I'd better go because my mom gets mad. She's visiting my aunt. Bye!"

"Bye."

Markus headed back to the projects. He planned to stop by Renata's and see what she was doing before going back to his apartment.

He didn't notice the car slam on brakes in front on him. Before his mind could process what was happening his dad jumped out the car and grabbed him, "So you wanna disrespect me? I need to teach you real good!"

He slammed Markus against the car, opened the door and threw him inside. John jumped behind the wheel and sped off. Markus didn't know where he was taking him, but he knew it wasn't going to be good for him.

24

Renata finished her homework and decided to study her Bible. She wanted to find the scripture about salvation to give it to Markus. She hoped she would be able to lead him to Christ.

Markus did not have the advantage of a true Christian home like she did. Her mother was strict but loving. She wanted to get Markus to trust God. She believed it was in his heart, but he just needed someone to guide him.

She took her time reading through different books her mother had in the apartment trying to find the answer. She knew what the answer was, but she wanted to show it to Markus in the Bible.

Her mom was downstairs talking to one of the neighbors about LaJuan. She felt horrible about that situation. She couldn't imagine the pain that LaJuan was living with every day.

She remembered the first time she met LaJuan how sad she looked. She thought maybe she had gotten into trouble with her parents, but now she realized it was far worse than that.

She stopped for a minute and prayed. She prayed that Markus would find God and that the two of them would someday start an organization to fight against family violence. She imagined their organization would be known around the world and help many people.

Her mom came in the room, "Hey baby, what are you doing?"

"Studying the word. I'm trying to find something for Markus."

She sat down, "Oh, what are you looking for?"

"The scripture that says what you have to do to be saved. I believe the pastor said it was Romans but I haven't found it yet."

Allison popped up, "Okay. I'm going to bed early. Good night."

Renata was surprised, "You're not going to tell me."

Allison stopped at the doorway, "Now if I did that, how would you learn? You're old enough now that if you have to find something in the word that you can do it yourself. You're in the right place; just have a little more determination and patience." She smiled and walked away.

Renata yelled, "Good night, Mom!"

"Good night, sweetheart!"

Renata loved her mother. They were mother and daughter as well as best friends. She often pushed Renata to learn for herself instead of taking the easy answer. This was another time; she would have to find the answer herself.

After searching for what seemed like hours, Renata found the answer. She felt very satisfied that she did it herself and that's what her mom wanted her to feel. She wrote 'Romans 10:9' on a piece of paper and rushed to the phone to call Markus.

She quickly dialed the number, and it rang. Damien answered, and Renata cringed, "Hi may I speak to Markus?"

"The punk ain't home, but you can always talk to me, baby. I got what you need."

Renata was repulsed, "No thank you. Please tell him I called." Damien didn't respond. He hung up the phone, and she nodded her head in disbelief. She decided to watch some TV and wait for Markus to call her back.

***

It was slightly after midnight when Renata woke up. She looked at the phone and realized that Markus did not call her back. She decided to pray. Markus always called her back, but she reasoned that Damien didn't tell him she called.

She decided to be bold and call him. She prayed his dad wouldn't answer the phone. His mom would probably be mad, but she wouldn't take it out on Markus.

Her prayers were answered, "Hello."

"Hi Mrs. Black is Markus awake."

She didn't respond so Renata asked again, "Mrs. Black, may I speak to Markus?"

She softly said, "I thought he was with you?"

Now Renata was worried, "No ma'am he left me hours ago. We came home from school and went to talk to Brittani then he went home. I haven't seen him since. Oh my God!"

Rhonda said, "His dad isn't home either. Maybe they're together." As bad as that idea was for Renata to think about she hoped that was true. At least he would be alive and hopefully safe.

"Okay, Mrs. Black. Please let me know when he's home. I know I won't be able to sleep."

"I will honey." She hung up the phone, and so did Renata. She started to wake her mom but decided against it. She just sat in the chair and quietly prayed for her boyfriend.

25

Markus didn't know exactly where he was, but his father stopped the car in a rundown part of town. The nearby buildings appear abandoned, but Markus could hear shouting.

His father got out the car and finished off a forty-ounce bottle he had been drinking. He opened Markus' door and dragged him out, "Now I'm gonna make a man out of you since that's what you think you are. You won't run from me anymore."

He pulled Markus along until they were inside one of the old abandoned building. People were standing around yelling, screaming, some were holding money in the air, and others were drinking.

Markus could see two men in the circle and they were fighting. One man had the other down on his knees, bloodied and beaten. He hit him one more time and knocks him out.

Markus was afraid. He feared his dad would put him out there to fight someone. He didn't understand why someone would do this to their son. He tried to love him like Renata said you should love everyone but this man was the epitome of evil.

John pulled Markus into one of the rooms away from the ring. Markus couldn't free himself of his grip. He threw Markus to the ground in front of three men, "This is my oldest son, and I need to make a man out of him tonight! I need one of you to toughen him up a bit. I got $100, who wants it?"

Markus tried to run but his dad grabbed him pulled him back. A man, the size of John, stepped up and said, "I'll handle it. I got one them too."

Markus said, "Dad, please, don't…"

"Listen to 'em, pleading like a girl."

The other men laughed. The man reared his fist back, and Markus closed his eyes. Before the punch landed, a commotion started outside the room.

The man dropped Markus to the ground, and they all peeked out the door. John said, "It's the police! We need to get out of here."

John grabbed Markus, but Markus fought back. He wasn't going to leave with him.

John pulled him close, "If you say one word to the police, I'll kill your mother."

Markus was afraid. He believed his dad.

The men climbed out of a window in the room. Markus continued to hear the commotion and it wasn't long before someone came into his room. It was a police officer, "Freeze!"

Markus didn't move. Out of fear he hadn't moved since his dad left. The officer realized that he was a kid, "What are you doing here son?"

Markus was too afraid to answer. He stayed there on his knees. Another officer came in the room, "What's going on here?"

"It's a kid. He won't say why he's here. What's your name son?"

Markus still wouldn't talk. The second officer said, "Take him downtown separately from everyone else. We'll see if he'll talk down there."

"Yes, sir. Come on son. It's going to be all right."

***

Markus was sitting in the police station afraid to say a word. He knew his father was evil and he believed that he would kill his mother if he told the police anything. He figured the best thing to do would be to not say anything.

The police officer who brought him into the station gave him some hot chocolate, "Here you go, son."

Markus smiled. He wanted to talk and started to talk. Before he could, he heard a familiar voice behind him.

"Yeah I'm his father."

Markus stood up and turned around. His father was approaching him.

John hugged him, "Son, where have you been? We've been looking everywhere for you. Your mom is worried to death."

The officer said, "We found his student ID on the ground at the building and called you. He hasn't said a word since we found him, so we don't know why he was down there."

John said, "Well we had to put him on punishment for fighting. He got mad and ran away." He put his arms around Markus, "I'll take him to his mother, and we'll sit down and talk it out like a Christian family."

The officer said, "Okay, Mr. Black. You'll have to sign some papers first and then we'll get you out of here."

John replied, "Thank you, officer."

The officer went to get the papers. John sat down next to Markus and whispered, "Good job. Keep this up, and I guess your mom will live to see another day."

He smiled so everyone in the room would think he was happy to see his son. Markus hated him. He wondered if he should do what LaJuan did. He didn't think he was as strong as her, but he secretly wished his father were dead.

***

Markus and his dad rode home mostly in silence. His dad made little comments threatening his mother's life if he were to talk. By this time Markus wasn't going to say anything to anyone. He had nothing to say to his father.

They went into the house, and Rhonda ran to Markus and hugged him, "Markus baby where have you been?"

Markus looked at his father, "I just ran away for a while, Momma. I'm sorry, I promise not to do it again."

His father smirked and went into the kitchen. Markus said, "I just want to go to sleep, Momma."

Rhonda replied, "Go ahead, darling. By the way, Renata called looking for you. She's really worried. Call her just in case she's still up."

"But mom it's two in the morning."

"She said she would be up because she wouldn't be able to sleep. She's worried about you. We all were."

"Okay, mom I'll call her right now." Markus went to the phone and dialed Renata's number. She answered right away, "Markus?"

"Yeah, baby it's me."

"Where in the world were you? I've been sitting here worried to death!"

"I'm sorry." John came and stood behind Markus. Markus glanced over his shoulder knowing he was there, "I just ran away. I needed some time to think. I hope you understand."

"I don't, and right now I'm pissed! You need to run away and make everyone worry about you! Good night Markus. Maybe I'll run away and think!" She angrily hung up the phone, and Markus felt horrible having to lie. He wished he could tell her the truth but his mom's life was at stake."

He gently hung up the phone and ran past his mom to his room. He hated his life. Now the only person aside from his mother and sister that loved him was angry with him. *"How can I make it up to her? I love her so much, but I had to lie to her, I had to."*

He quietly cried until he fell asleep, hoping that when the sun rose, the next morning everything would be better.

***

It was morning. Markus didn't get much sleep, but he didn't care. He needed to get dressed and down to Renata's house. He prayed that he could fix it. He loved her so much, and the thought of her being mad at him was killing him.

He got dressed and ran downstairs. Rhonda said, "Honey eat some breakfast."

Markus replied, "No time, Momma." He turned and snatched a piece of toast from Kyanna and kept running."

He heard Kyanna say, "Hey! Momma, he took my toast."

Markus yelled, "Sorry, Ky!" He darted down the grass and sidewalk area passed the rows of apartments until he got to Renata's."

He banged on the door like it was an emergency. To him, it was an emergency. Allison answered the door, "Hi Markus. Renata's already gone."

His heart dropped. Since they had been dating she had never left for the bus without him. He knew she was really angry. Allison said, "Give her some time Markus. She was really worried about you and to find out you simply ran away without consulting her...well, that hurt her very much."

Markus was fighting back the tears. Allison must have noticed. She stepped out the door and hugged Markus, "It's gonna be okay son. Trust me. She'll come around."

"Okay, Mrs. Smith. I'd better go before I miss the bus."

He really didn't want to go to the bus stop. She was angry and might not want anything to do with him. That would be hard and not to mention embarrassing. He wondered if he should tell her but dismissed the thought because his mom's life was at stake.

He got to the bus stop, and Renata was standing with Andra, Paula, and Shelia. *"At least she's not with another guy."*

Cleveland stepped up to Markus, "Man what happened? Did you and Renata break up?"

"I don't think so, I guess I'm about to find out."

"Good luck bro."

Markus walked over to them. He wondered if he should hug Renata. He was scared to try because she might not respond. He thought, *"Oh well, nothing beats a failure..."*

He hugged her, and she hugged him back. He felt a great relief that she didn't embarrass him. Markus said, "I'm sorry baby. How can I make it up to you?"

Renata looked at him, and it was apparent that she was mad. Andra said, "You can speak to the rest of us? I know Y'all got drama but come on."

Markus said, "Oh good morning ladies." They all said good morning back to him.

Renata replied, "Markus, I'm still mad at you. You just don't get it. I'm your girlfriend, and you can't lock me out like that. I want to be here for you but you pushing me away isn't going to help."

"Renata you just don't understand."

"Make me understand!"

The bus pulled up, and everyone was getting on except Markus and Renata. The couple stood there arguing until the bus driver blew his horn.

They got on the bus, and everyone was laughing at them. In a way, Markus liked all the attention, but it was for the wrong reason. How could he make her understand without telling her the truth?

26

Damien stood behind the apartments waiting on the bus from Adams to arrive. He wanted to talk to Brittani, but if he waited in the open, she might make a scene.

The bus pulled up to the 22nd Street stop, and the kids started to get off the bus. He watched until he saw Brittani get off. He ran over, "Brittani."

She was startled and jumped behind a friend. Damien said, "Brittani let me talk to you."

"No Damien. I have nothing to say to you. Leave me alone."

"Come on Brittani let me explain."

Brittani's friend Teddy stepped in, "Hey man she said, 'leave her alone.' Can't you hear?"

Damien sternly replied, "Back off, Teddy."

Brittani turned and ran. Damien shouted, "Brittani wait!"

Teddy grabbed Damien by the arm and by instinct Damien turned and struck him in the face. The blow knocked Teddy backward and Damien struck him twice more in the face. Teddy fell to one knee, and Damien kicked him in the chest and stomped him before some of the boys pulled him off of him. Damien put his hands on his head and ran toward Brittani's house.

He got to Brittani's house and knocked on the door. No one answered. He knocked again and again but got no answer.

He was angry and stormed back to his apartment. She wouldn't have anything to do with him. That was not acceptable. His dad would not accept that. He had to handle his business.

***

Damien was talking to two of his closest friends. He was still fuming that Brittani wouldn't talk to him. Nate and Don always hung out with Damien. The three of them got into trouble all the time.

Nate said, "I can't believe she disrespected you like that. You need to put her in her place brother."

Don added, "Yeah she needs a lesson."

Damien didn't respond. He was angry, and he missed LaJuan. He hated her for years, but she stole his heart in two days. He planned to go see her over the weekend.

Nate poked Damien in the arm, "Yo man what's up?"

Damien said, "What? I was just thinking about what I need to do. I miss LaJuan."

Don replied, "What? Man, what did she do to you?"

"Bro you just don't know. She was magical. I'm glad she took out her parents especially her stepdad, but I wish she was still here. I can use some of that stuff."

Don said, "It was that good?"

"Oh yeah man."

Nate replied, "Forget that, what are you going to do about Brittani?"

Don responded, "You should just leave her alone. She can be trouble. Her mom ain't no joke."

Damien sternly said, "My dad can handle her easily. I'm going to see if she answers the door."

Nate replied, "All right man. We'll be right here when you get back."

Don responded, "Yeah bro good luck."

Damien got up and headed to Brittani's house. He missed LaJuan, but he still wanted Brittani. The more she ignored him, the angrier he got.

He got to Brittani's apartment, and she was standing outside with some friends. She saw Damien and she went back to her apartment. Damien got there, and all her friends blocked the door preventing Damien from getting to Brittani.

Cheryl said, "Go away. No one wants you here Damien."

Damien assessed the situation and felt it was too many of them to start anything. He decided to leave. He was angry the rest of the night, but he had no hold on Brittani. He visualized that if he was a big time A&R man with a music company he could get all the women he wanted. They would stay with him because they would want a record deal. If the men in suits weren't lying, he would get that position. He vowed he would use it to his advantage.

27

Markus had the worst day. Renata wouldn't talk to him, and it hurt him deeply. He had to find a way to fix it, but all he could come up with was to tell her the truth. That truth could cost his mom her life. At some point, he realized that if he loved Renata and she loved him, he would have to trust her with his secret.

He pondered the thought all day and intensely debated it in his head during his last period. She was his girl, and she showed that she loved him. However, her mom did call the social worker on them so could he really trust her with his mother's life? Would she believe that his dad was capable of killing his mom?

He knew without a doubt that his dad would follow through with the threat but Renata may not understand as he did. School let out, and he made the seemingly long walk to the bus. He knew she would still be mad at him, so it was going to be an excruciatingly long ride back home.

He got to the bus and took his seat by Renata. He looked at her, and she smiled at him. He was happy that she at least smiled at him. That was a good start.

He asked, "What you writing?"

She answered, "The reasons why I love you."

"What? Are you really writing that?"

She smiled again, "Yes. I don't want to continue fighting with you, but you don't seem to understand my feelings for you. You don't understand that I stayed up all night waiting to hear from you because I was worried. Have you ever been like that? Have you ever sat up and waited for someone because you were worried about them? It's not a great feeling, especially when they have no good reason for doing what they did."

Markus knew he had to tell her now. He couldn't continue to let this go on. He had to put his trust in her and tell her what happened the night before. He couldn't do it on the bus, so he planned to do it on the walk home.

Renata continued, "I know you're in a difficult situation and I'm trying to understand it but I can't because you don't want to talk about it. However, I will respect your decision and wait for you to trust me enough to let me in. I love you that much."

Markus felt guilty for sure now. She was giving more to the relationship than he would have ever expected her to do. He had to tell her and pray that she would keep it to herself. He would ask her not to tell her mom either.

He held her hand, "Baby, I will open up more to you. Just understand that for years I only had me and no one else. This relationship thing is all new to me."

"It's new to me too Markus. You're my first boyfriend."

"I know, but you have a happy life, a happy home and a lot of friends. I don't have any of that. I have a couple of friends, and that's it."

Renata laid her head on Markus' shoulder, "I know sweetie, but that's all changed now. I'm your best friend." She looked up at him and smiled then she caressed his chin.

Markus felt good. The bus pulled up to their stop, and Markus and Renata got off. Their friends surrounded them as they walked home, so Markus didn't get a chance to tell Renata.

Once they got to the front porch, Renata noticed her mom wasn't home. She said, "Momma gone. That's unusual. Wanna come in?"

"Sure."

Renata smiled sarcastically, "Don't get no ideas; it's not that kind of party baby."

Markus laughed, "Oh I knew that. Don't you know that I know my baby by now?"

"I sure hope you do. I'm a Christian and proud of it. Not to mention I'm only 16. So are you sweetie."

Markus calmly replied, "There's no rush."

Renata replied, "See...that's why I love you. We right here." She pointed from her eyes to his eyes.

Markus said, "Can we sit down and talk."

Renata's look changed, "Do you want something to drink first?"

"No thank you."

Renata sat down on the couch, and Markus sat next to her and looked seriously into the eyes. He didn't know how to start so he would just tell her about the incident from the day before.

"Renata, what I'm about to tell you must stay between you and me. My mother's life depends on it. So please, don't tell it to anyone, not even your mom."

Renata's face turned serious, "Okay Markus, I promise not to tell anyone."

Markus deeply sighed, "Yesterday when I got home my dad started on me. He wanted to beat me for fighting Damien which I actually didn't. We never actually had a fight; I just stopped him from abusing Brittani."

"Well, I was so angry that once again my happiness was taken away from me by the man that I ran out the house and didn't stop until I got to Young. I stayed there for a minute, and then I decided to come back to you."

"As you know I never made it. He pulled on 22nd and dragged me into his car. He took me to some place where people were taking bets and fighting. He wanted one of his friends to 'teach me a lesson on toughness.'"

"Before the man could beat on me the police came and raided the place. They took me to the station where I sat for hours until my dad picked me up. He escaped when the police came in on the raid."

"Before he left the room I was in, he told me if I said a word to anyone that he would kill my mother. I believe him, I believe he will kill my mother so please, please don't tell anyone." Tears were forming in Markus' eyes, but he was trying to hold them back.

Renata's head dropped in disbelief, "What kind of monster would do that to his own son? Oh my God." She put her hand to her face, and a tear rolled down her cheek.

Markus put his arm around her and held her tightly, "You see baby, I didn't tell you because I'm afraid of what might happen to my mom. It's not that I don't trust you, I do, but we're talking about my mom."

"I understand Markus, and I'm nowhere near mad at you anymore. In fact, I'm sorry that I was ever mad at you."

She started to kiss him when her mother walked in the front door. Allison stood at the door by the stairs staring at both of them, "Now you know...I don't allow you to have boys in this house when I'm not home. Have you lost your mind?"

Renata tried to conceal her tears and frustration, "I'm sorry mom. Markus was just leaving. He just had something to tell me real quick. Next time we'll sit on the front porch."

"You darn right you will. Don't let this happen again."

Markus said, "Yes ma'am."

Renata joined him, "Yes ma'am."

Markus got up and walked out the apartment. He had just shared one of the most important secrets in his life to Renata. He knew he loved her and he trusted her not to tell. Now he dreaded going home.

***

Markus got home, and his mom and dad were dancing in the living room. Even Kyanna was happy and laughing at them. These were the times that were deceiving to anyone watching. You would think their home was a happy home, but this always happened after his dad had beaten someone earlier. He would always find a way to convince his mom that he was sorry and wanted to change.

Markus said under his breath, *"What a farce."* He went upstairs and to his room. He was happy that Damien wasn't home. He hated having to share a room with him, especially since he had changed so much. Their opinions were extremely opposite now.

Kyanna came running into the room, "Markus, guess what I got?"

"What did you get?"

"I got an 'A' on my math test! I did exactly what you said, and I aced that joint!"

Markus said, "Yeah!" Markus high-fived his baby sister.

Kyanna replied, "Oh, mom wants you."

"Okay." Markus didn't want to go back downstairs, but he had to go see what his mom wanted. He walked down the stairs behind his baby sister. He did love seeing her happy. She deserved to be happy.

Rhonda said, "Hey Markus, I made your favorite meal. Come on and let's eat as a family tonight."

Markus didn't want to eat as a family because they weren't a family. At least they weren't a happy one. They all heard the knock at the front door, and Kyanna ran to open it.

Markus nearly passed out when he saw Renata come inside, "Hey what brings you here?"

"You always come to my house, so I decided to visit you. Is this a bad time?"

Markus didn't know what to say, "Um..."

Rhonda chimed in, "Come on in and have dinner with us."

Renata said, "I don't want to impose."

John replied, "Nonsense sit down and eat with us. It nice to see the young lady my oldest son chose to fall in love with."

His comments disgusted Markus. It was all show and even more now that Renata was here. He didn't care for her at all, and now he was pretending to be a nice person.

Markus held the chair for Renata, and she sat down.

John said, "Well look at that Rhonda, we have a true gentleman in the house."

Markus sarcastically commented, "That's how you treat someone you love."

Renata put her hand on Markus' hand. He knew she didn't want him to start trouble and he realized that he didn't want her in the midst of it either.

They all enjoyed dinner, and the show continued until Renata left. Markus didn't know what to expect after he came back from walking her home but he knew it would be something.

He came back in the apartment to find Damien laying on the couch and Kyanna lying on the floor. Their parents were nowhere to be found.

Markus asked, "Where's mom and dad?"

Kyanna answered, "Upstairs with the door closed."

Markus hoped that mean he wouldn't see his dad anymore that night. He asked Kyanna, "Ky, You wanna play checkers?"

"Yeah!"

28

Visiting hours at the jail started at 10. Damien took two buses to get down there so he could visit LaJuan. He truly missed her and wanted to see her badly. He checked in at the front desk and waited for her to come out.

When she came out in her orange prison suit, Damien's heart throbbed. She was beautiful to him even in jail attire.

LaJuan eased down in the chair and picked up the phone. She didn't smile at all. Damien picked up the phone, "Hey LaJuan. You doing okay?"

"Do I look okay?"

Damien was shocked at the response. He thought she would be glad to see him, but he wasn't getting that feeling, "What's wrong baby?"

"What's wrong? I'm in jail, and you're enjoying life. I shouldn't have listened to you. Why did you come visit me?"

"LaJuan, I realize that I love you and I miss you."

She hung up the phone and walked away. Damien sat there in disbelief. She had changed. The few days in jail had already turned her heart, and she blamed Damien for it.

Damien held the phone to his ear for a few minutes before he realized that he should hang it up and leave.

Damien stood on the street corner, confused and hurt. He waited all week to go see this girl and she shut him out. She was cold and heartless toward him.

The two bus rides back to Belmont Heights seemed to take an eternity. Damien thought long and hard on the ride. He was failing miserably at being like his dad. If his dad found out how women were disrespecting him, he would beat him to a pulp. He had to show the world that he was not to be disrespected.

29

It was Sunday morning, and Markus was excited. He was going to church with Renata, and he felt good about it. They talked the day before for hours about Jesus, and Markus felt ready to turn his life over to Christ. He would do it today. He would go in front of the church and tell them that he wanted to be saved.

He walked out the apartment and headed down to Renata's apartment, but before he got far, Allison pulled up in her car. Markus jumped in the backseat, and they headed to church.

Allison, Renata, and Markus sat near the front of the church. Markus held Renata's hand. The children's choir marched in from the rear of the church, and Markus saw his little friend, Raine.

Raine waved at Markus and Markus smiled and waved back. Renata looked at him and whispered, "Should I be worried?"

Markus laughed, "No baby, I think she's a little young for me."

They both giggled.

When Raine sang her solo, the entire church was amazed. She was natural. Markus marveled at her talent.

It finally reached the moment for Markus to make his decision. He didn't want to wait, and as soon as the pastor invited people to give their life to Christ, he was going to go up there.

The pastor made his usual invitation and Markus pushed past Renata and Allison to the isle then to the front of the church. He was so excited he never realized that Renata followed him.

He looked back and smiled when he realized that his girlfriend was supporting him. The ministry asked him why he was up front and he told him he wanted to be baptized. Renata was smiling and just as excited as Markus.

After the service, Allison said, "Well we need to celebrate this! Let's go get something to eat."

They both were excited and happy. Markus had never experienced such happiness in his life. He was now a Christian man with a Christian girlfriend who loved him as much as he loved her.

***

Markus came running into the apartment with Renata right behind him. The rain was coming down hard outside, and they were trying to beat it.

Markus laughed, "I beat you!"

"Cause you cheated."

"What? You just slow baby."

"Whatever...can a sister get a towel?"

Kyanna said, "I'll get it!"

John came from upstairs. Markus feared the worse. Kyanna came back with the towel, "Here you go."

"Thank you, Ky. Hi, Mr. Black."

John said, "Hi." He kept walking like she really wasn't there.

Markus asked Kyanna, "Where's mom?"

"Right here baby." Rhonda came down the stairs, "Hey Renata. How are you, sweetie?"

"I'm good, Mrs. Black, how are you?"

"Well I'm here so I guess I'm good. How was church?"

Renata looked at Markus. Markus smiled at his mom, "Momma I got saved today! I'm a Christian!"

Rhonda excitedly replied, "What, that's wonderful Markus!"

Rhonda and Kyanna hugged Markus. Renata added, "I'm so excited for him Mrs. Black."

"What the Hell you mean you're a Christian? Who told you to make that decision without consulting me?" John shouted from the kitchen.

He marched in the living room with a beer in his hand and stared at Markus and Renata.

Rhonda said, "Now John..."

"Shut up." He turned to Renata, "I think you need to leave young lady. You've caused enough commotion here today."

Markus hugged Renata and whispered in her ear, "It's okay." He kissed her on the cheek. Fear was evident on her face. Markus didn't want her exposed to the violent side of his family, and he encouraged her to leave.

It was still pouring outside, and Kyanna handed her an umbrella, "Here, Renata. You can use my umbrella."

Renata smiled, and Kyanna smiled back, but it was more fear than joy. They all knew the next few moments were going to be difficult.

Renata was gone, and now it was time to face the music. Rhonda tried to calm the situation down, "John, the boy, has to make this decision on his own and we should respect that decision."

He grabbed her by the throat, "If I have to tell you to shut up again I know something!" He pushed her back and pointed at Markus.

Kyanna started to cry. John shouted at her, "Get upstairs now!"

Kyanna ran upstairs. Markus braced himself. He was not going to bow down to him this time. This time he believed he had the backing of God and that nothing this man did to him would succeed.

"So you think you're saved now? You think God is with you?" John slapped Markus across the face, but Markus didn't step back. He had enough of the abuse and wasn't going to back down from his decision.

"Oh, you're a man."

Markus said, "Yes and a bigger one than you!"

John tried to punch Markus, but Rhonda stepped between them and took the blow. She quickly fell to the ground, and Markus shouted, "I hate you!" He dove at John catching him in the waist area.

Markus began punching profusely at his dad's face until he was yanked backward. Markus looked up, and Damien pulled him off their dad. Damien then kicked Markus several times in the side.

Upstairs John heard Kyanna calling the police. John stood up and grabbed Damien. He led Damien out the door.

Markus crawled over to his mom. She was unconscious. Kyanna ran down the stairs crying.

Markus told her, "Go next door and get Mrs. Rosy." She did.

30

Today was LaJuan's arraignment. She sat
in her cell waiting to go to the courtroom.
Her court-appointed lawyer advised her
to plead guilty by reason of insanity,
something LaJuan didn't want to do.

As she sat there waiting to be escorted to
court, she pondered her situation. She
wondered how she got to this point, how
could she be facing time in jail, maybe for
life, after being raped and abused
repeatedly? She said, *"Life sucks, and then
you die!"*

She looked up, and the same two men in
suits she met at her mom's job were being
let into her cell. She wondered if she
would ever see them again.

The same man that spoke before spoke
again, "Are you okay? Is there anything
we can get you?"

LaJuan giggled, "Yeah, you can get me out
of here."

The man didn't crack a smile. Instead, he
looked at the guard, "Leave us now." The

guard didn't say a word he just walked off and left them there alone with LaJuan.

LaJuan had thoughts of being raped again. She was not comfortable being alone with adult men. After all, the man who was supposed to protect her was the one who was doing the raping and abusing.

She was scared. She didn't have a weapon to defend herself, and it was two of them. She stood up and moved as far back as she could in the cell.

The man said, "We're not here to harm you. In fact, we want you to work for us."

LaJuan laughed, "Really, how can I do that? I'm going to prison for killing my rapist and his accomplice."

"We will have the charges dropped, and in return, you will work for us, for life. You will want for nothing, and you will be in the best of care. No one will harm you again. We will train you and provide you with a home to live in."

LaJuan didn't understand what was happening. She said, "I'm only 14, not even old enough to work."

"You won't be required to work right away. The next four years you will spend getting your education like any other student. After that, we will train you. You will work for us for now on."

"So they will just drop all the charges against me?"

"Yes, as long as you agree to our terms."

"Okay, let's do it."

The second man pulled out a knife and handed it to the first man. LaJuan said, "Whoa, hold on a minute."

The first man said, "We will not harm you. Our contracts are signed in blood and for life. Hold out your right hand."

LaJuan complied, and the man took the knife and cut a slit in the palm of LaJuan's hand. She expected it to hurt, but she felt no pain.

The second man then handed the first man a piece of paper. The first man took LaJuan's hand stamped it on the paper. He then did the same thing with his hand.

Afterwards, he said, "It is done. When the judge asks you 'how do you plead,' you say 'not guilty.' We will see you after court."

Without any emotion, they turned and walked out the cell. The guard came and escorted LaJuan to court.

***

LaJuan's turn in the courtroom finally came. She looked around, but she didn't see the men in suits. Her attorney wasn't even in the courtroom. She didn't know what was going on, but she was nervous. She didn't understand what the signing in blood meant, but she didn't care because she was getting off for murdering her parents.

The bailiff said, "All rise, the case of LaJuan Craig versus the State of Florida is now in session. The Honorable Judge William Cochran is presiding."

The judge stated, "Young lady you're facing one count of premeditated murder in the first degree and one count of murder in the first degree, how do you plead."

LaJuan did as the man said, "Not guilty."

He asked the assistant district attorney, "Mrs. Thompson, what do you say?"

Mrs. Thompson answered, "Your honor in light of the circumstances surrounding this case we feel it is in the best interest of all parties that the charges be dropped, and Ms. Craig be turned over to the Baal Reformatory School for Girls."

The judge read over some papers then replied, "I agree Mrs. Thompson. The charges are dropped, and Ms. Craig will be placed in the care of the Baal Reformatory School for Girls until she is 18 years old. Case dismissed."

LaJuan stood up. She didn't know what to do. An older woman approached her, "Come with me."

LaJuan thought her voice was cold and heartless. She didn't know what was going to be expected of her, but anything was better than jail for the rest of her life.

31

Markus sat by his mother's bedside at Saint Joseph Hospital. The doctors, nurses, and police all tried to get him to say what happened the day before. They even tried to get Kyanna to talk. Markus thought how they all had been trained to never tell anyone what was happening in their home. Their dad had total control even when he wasn't around.

Markus was proud of himself for standing up to his dad. He firmly believed it was his new found Christianity that gave him the courage. He looked over at Kyanna. She had spent the night at the hospital also. Neither of them wanted to go home.

His mom was waking up. The bruise on her face was nasty, and it made Markus even angrier when he looked at it.

Rhonda asked, "Where am I?"

"You're in Saint Joseph's mom. You hit your head on the coffee table."

"Where's your dad and brother?"

Markus frowned, "Hell I hope."

Rhonda looked at him sternly, "Don't ever say that again. You're a Christian now, and you can't wish death on anyone."

"Yes, ma'am."

Rhonda looked over at Kyanna, "Ky...wake up baby."

Kyanna was still sleeping. Markus said, "She was up late hoping you would wake up."

"Oh my baby, what did you tell the police?

Markus sighed, "That you tripped and fell. When you did, you hit your head on the coffee table. Mom, no one believes those lies. We should tell the truth."

"No baby, please don't start okay?"

Rhonda sat up on the bed, "I need to get out of here. Go get the doctor for me."

"Okay, mom."

32

Renata was worried about Markus. She hadn't heard from him since they got home from church and his father was upset that he had given his life to Christ. Renata wondered how anyone could be upset that a person chooses to better their life by serving Christ.

She quickly got up and dressed. She went downstairs and dialed Markus' number, but Damien answered, "Hello."

"Hi, is Markus in?"

"No baby but if you want to trade up, I can be there in a flash."

Renata hung up the phone. She didn't like Damien at all, and it took a lot for her to dislike someone. She wondered if Markus would even come to school.

The phone rang, and Renata quickly answered, "Hello."

Markus said, "Hey sweetheart."

"Hey, Markus I just tried to call you. Are you okay?"

"Yeah I'm cool. I'm at the hospital with my mom. I won't be at school today."

Renata covered her mouth, "Oh my God, is she okay?"

"Yeah, she's going to be fine."

"Did he hit her?"

There was a pause and Renata knew he didn't want to answer. She continued, "You don't have to answer that. I know he's probably around."

"Yep. I hope you have a good day at school and remember who your BF is?"

Renata laughed, "Really Markus, I think about my BF all the time so I can't forget who he is okay."

Markus said, "I'm just joking around."

"I know baby. Well, I have to run out to catch the bus. Call me tonight."

"I will. Have a blessed day sweetheart."

"You too, baby."

She hung up the phone, knelt down and prayed for Markus and his family. She wanted to do something for them, but she knew she couldn't until Markus decided he wanted to do something. If she took any steps now, it would just drive a wedge between them, and she didn't want that.

Renata kissed her mom and ran out the door to the bus stop. She ran into her friend Andra, and they walked together. Renata said, "You know I made a good decision in dating Markus. He's a great catch."

Andra smiled, "You're a great catch too you know."

Renata posed, "Well what can I say?"

They both laughed. Andra put her hand on Renata's arm, "Girl guess who asked me to the movies Saturday?"

Renata said, "Who?"

"Guess girl?"

"Come on Andra, tell me?"

Andra replied, "Okay, Omar."

They both laughed, and Renata said, "It's about time! What was he waiting for girl?"

"I don't have any idea, but he said he wasn't sure I liked him." She smirked, "Come on I was throwing every hint at you, but I wasn't going to do all the work for you. He who findeth..."

Renata replied, "Well I did put in a little more work than I should have with Markus but if I hadn't he would never have talked to me."

"Well, that was different given his situation."

"You know what's amazing Andra? Everyone knows what his family is going through, but it's a secret. How can something be a secret but everyone knows about it? I mean really."

Andra took a deep breath, "Well, it's a secret that everyone in Belmont Heights knows it but they won't report it to the authorities. They believe it's a family matter, so the secret is from the authorities not each other."

"Good point. I want to help him, but he's got to want help. He doesn't want to do anything because of his mom. I can understand that but still they need help."

Andra said seriously, "Don't push it. Just be there when he's ready for you."

"I will be girl. Thanks for that. It's hard to watch it. Yesterday his dad got mad and kicked me out the house because Markus became a Christian. Isn't that just stupid?"

"Oh my God, Markus got saved! That's wonderful!"

"I know right. I was so happy for him."

Andra said, "So his dad got upset and threw you out? That's crazy."

Renata angrily replied, "Yes, really crazy. I can't stand that man. I know we're taught to love our enemies, but this is crazy."

Andra responded, "Yeah it is crazy but just keep praying for them. Something happens when we call His name."

"Amen to that my sister."

***

It was a long day for Renata. All she could think of was Markus and what he was doing. The bus pulled up, and she quickly went home, dropped her books off and went down to Markus' apartment.

When she arrived, she realized she should have called first because Damien might be home by himself and she didn't want to see him. She calmly knocked on the door, and Markus answered.

Renata smiled, "Hey sweetie!"

He came out the door, smiled and hugged her tightly, "Hey baby. How was your day?"

"Okay, I couldn't help but wonder if you were okay. Are you?"

Markus twisted his lips, "Yeah I'm cool. You know how it is here."

"I do Markus, and you know my position on this. Tell somebody."

Markus turned his head. Renata said, "Okay, okay...when you're ready, then I'll be ready."

Markus nodded, "Okay. Anything happened at school?"

Renata answer, "Nothing really. It was just the same old boring day at school. Oh, Andra might be getting a boyfriend. She and Omar are going out Saturday."

Markus' eyebrow went up, "Really, I don't really know that guy."

"He's cool. I've met him a few times. He's into the arts."

Markus replied, "That sounds cool."

Renata asked, "How's your mom?"

Markus answered, "She's good. They let her come home, and she's in there cooking." Markus heard his dad yell something to Kyanna.

He looked pitifully at Renata, "I should go."

Renata hugged him, and they kissed.

John shouted, "Markus!"

Markus let go of Renata, "Bye Renata." He turned and walked inside before Renata could respond.

She stood there for a second before she decided to leave. She loved him, and she felt she was hurt when he was hurt. She could tell he was hurting right now.

33

Damien stood on the corner when the limo pulled up in front of him. The window rolled down, and the man in the suit motioned for him to get in the limo. Damien hesitated but then got inside.

The two men nodded to the driver and the limo drove off. Damien was scared. He tried not to show it. He didn't know what these men wanted with him, but if they wanted to kill him, there wouldn't be anything he could do about it.

They rode in quiet. The limo left the city limits and to a place that Damien didn't recognize. There was only one building that stood auspiciously by itself.

The limo went through the gate and down the long road to the building. It stopped in front of the building, and the driver opened the limo door. The man motioned for Damien to get out the limo.

He did, and the place was eerie. It was broad daylight when Damien was picked up, but somehow the sun didn't shine in this place.

The men led Damien inside the building down a long hallway. He got on the evaluator and went to the top floor.

The doors opened, and there were several people working in cubicles. Damien walked passed them noting that no one paid any attention to him.

He walked in a room that was a conference room, and a man was sitting at the end of the conference room table. Damien couldn't make out his face because the lighting in the room was dim.

The man said, "You're Damien Black?"

Damien was scared but managed to answer, "Yes."

The man continued, "It is my understanding that you desire to be a music industry artist and repertoire man. Is this true?"

Damien perked up, "Yes sir! That's my dream."

The man continued seemly calm to Damien, "Do you ever wonder how stars are made?"

"Yeah well they are discovered by an AR man. If he thinks they got talent, then he can get them a record deal."

The man let out an eerie laugh, "No my little friend. We make them stars. We put plans into place years ahead of time to make people a success. Your father could have been a success, but your mother got in the way. That's why he hates her today. You are special. You have followed in your father's footsteps, and we have paved the way for you to be a success. Do you want it?"

"Yes, I want to be a star."

"We will make you the most popular A/R man in the business. You'll finish your education then come work for us at Fresh City Records. You will get the talent we want to sign and make them into stars. Is this agreeable?"

Damien was excited, "Yes, but my parents won't let me do that."

"Don't worry about your parents. Are you ready to sign your contract?"

Damien was confused, "My contract? I'm not old enough to sign a contract."

The man continued, "You are old enough to enter into this contract. Remember our contracts are for life. You sign with us, and you'll have more money than you ever wanted for the rest of your life."

Damien asked, "But what about my parents?"

The man said coldly, "Take him away from me!"

"No, wait, I'll sign...I'll sign!"

The man slid a piece of paper in front of Damien. The man who brought Damien into the room took his hand and pulled out a black blade with jagged edges. He stabbed the tip of the blade into the palm of Damien's hand and cut his fingers.

Damien let out a scream as the blood from his hand dripped onto the document. It appeared to boil and dry in front of Damien's eyes.

The other man handed Damien a towel. The first man handed the document to the man at the end of the table. He pulled out a knife and slit the palm of his hand. He made a fist, and the blood dripped to the document.

He said, "It is done."

***

The limo let Damien off around the corner from his apartment. He walked slowly home. He looked at his hand it was completely healed. Damien saw something lying on the ground in front of him. He reached down and picked it up. It was a wad of bills totaling six hundred and sixty-six dollars.

Damien was excited. He shouted, "Yes, I'm rich!" He ran home to show his mom and dad. When he got there, his dad was on the warpath again, so he decided not to say anything.

He walked in and past the shouting to the kitchen. He didn't care what happened to them because he believed his life was planned out and all taken care of now.

Damien heard his dad slap his mom across the face. She hit the ground hard, and Damien snickered. He said to himself, *"Should've let him be an A/R like me. That's what you get!"*

He had no feelings for what was happening to his mom. Damien just sat down and ate his dinner like he didn't have a care in the world.

34

LaJuan was in her new bedroom in her new home. She never imagined that she would be living in such an immaculate house. She didn't know how many bedrooms were in this house, but she stopped counting at ten.

She hadn't allowed herself to get close to anyone else living there. Her short friendship with Damien ended with her facing life in jail because she listened to him. She didn't know if she would have killed her parents anyway, but Damien inspired her to do it, so he was at fault. She thought she should have killed him too.

She couldn't believe she had sex with him. That day it was great, but now the thought of it disgusted her. Her thoughts were interrupted by the knock at the door, "Come in," she said.

The woman who brought LaJuan to the house came in the room. She sat down on the bed next to LaJuan. For the first time, LaJuan saw her smile, "How are you adjusting to your new life?"

LaJuan managed to smile, "It's good so far. When can I see my aunt? She was the only one who cared about me."

"I'm afraid that you won't be able to see her again. Your new life means that you have to leave all the old life behind, even the good things."

That news didn't make LaJuan happy. She cared about her aunt, and she wanted to see her again. However, she was afraid of what would happen to her if she crossed these people. They had the power to get her murder charges dropped and put her in this big mansion.

She said, "Okay. What am I expected to do?"

"You will learn everything over the next four years." She threw her head back and smiled again. LaJuan thought the smile was evil and wicked. She was really afraid now. She continued, "For now you will be expected to get all the education you can. When you're 18, you will begin your training for your job."

LaJuan asked, "What if I fail at it?"

She snickered, "Somehow I don't think you will. You are very talented. You killed your parents with ease. I think you'll fit right in with our organization."

She turned and walked out of LaJuan's bedroom. LaJuan didn't know what that 'fit right in' comment meant, but it must have something to do with killing people. She wondered if she was going to be an assassin or something. She blew off the thought thinking that was crazy, after all, she was just a kid.

***

LaJuan was sitting on the porch of the mansion when one of the other girls sat down next to her. The girl said, "Hi, I'm Porshia. What's your name?"

Reluctantly she answered, "LaJuan, LaJuan Craig."

"Well, LaJuan what did you do to get here?"

LaJuan didn't understand, "What do you mean?"

"We all have a story, a story that ended us up here. These people prey on our story, offer us this amazing life but what you don't know is that it comes with a price."

"What's the price?"

"Hmmmm...you haven't been here long enough to trust."

LaJuan stared at the girl, "I killed my parents."

"Whoa, that's a big one. Why?"

LaJuan sternly asked, "What's your story?"

Porshia answered, "Okay, well a couple of years ago my boyfriend got me strung out on heroin. I was so strung out that I dropped out of school and I was headed down. I probably would have died if the men in suits hadn't come along and saved me."

LaJuan said, "My stepfather was raping me, so I killed him."

Porshia's head went back, "Well he deserved it. That must have been hard on you."

"It was. I hated life."

Porshia smiled, "Well life here is great, but I hope you're up to the task."

"What is the task?"

"I can't go into that with you. You see you're still just a little kid. I graduate this year, and I can't mess things up for me. Just do what you're told to do without question and you'll be fine."

LaJuan was emotionless. Porshia got up and walked away. LaJuan really wanted to call her aunt. She got up and looked around the house to find a phone.

There wasn't one in sight. She wondered, *"Who has a house without a phone?"*

She continued looking until she saw the head of the house in his office talking on the phone. LaJuan just walked by wondering if she should ask or sneak in the office when he wasn't there.

One of the girls walked by her and LaJuan asked, "They're no phones here?"

The girl responded dryly, "Who are you going to call? They don't want you contacting anyone from your old life so...no."

"I guess you have a point. Thanks."

She kept going, and LaJuan decided to wait around and pray that he leave his office. She would sneak into the office and make a quick call to her aunt just to let her know she's okay.

***

She must have waited for two hours before the man left his office. LaJuan caught a break because he didn't lock the office door. LaJuan waited a few seconds then she crept into the office.

The phone was sitting on the large mahogany desk. It was a fancy phone, fancier than any phone LaJuan had ever seen.

She quickly dialed her aunt and patiently waited for her to answer. She did, "Hello."

LaJuan whispered, "Hey Auntie, this is LaJuan."

Aunt Carol replied, "LaJuan, where are you? I came to the courthouse, but they wouldn't let me in. They said it was a private session."

"I don't know exactly where I am, but I'm okay. The judge dismissed my charges and…" She heard someone approaching, "Auntie I have to go…I'm at the Baal Reformatory School for…"

The line went dead, and LaJuan quickly hung up. She ran and hid behind a bookcase. Two men came in to survey the room. She knew they were looking for her and hoped they couldn't see where she was hiding.

They left the room, and LaJuan tipped out. She ran as fast as she could down the hall and up the stairs to her room. She quickly went in and closed the door in fear.

At least she got to talk to her aunt and let her know she was safe. That was better than nothing at all.

35

Markus was upset. His dad slapped his mom to the ground after she had just got out the hospital. He knew this had to end and despite what his mom said in the past he was going to tell someone. He was going, to tell the truth about what was going on in the Black's home.

Unknown to anyone Markus had the number for Mrs. Boykin. He pulled it out of his secret hiding place and put it in his pocket. He had to call her from a phone booth, so he went downstairs.

His dad towered over his mother again. She was on the floor sobbing. Thankfully, Kyanna wasn't home at all.

Markus stood there looking at his dad. John said, "What the hell you looking at? Get in there and wash the dishes!"

"It's Damien's..."

"I told you to do it! Now get in there!"

Markus was angry. Even when he decided to take some action his father still managed to stop it from happening. *"Did he have ESP or something?"*

The phone rang, and John answered it, "Hello." He paused to listen then responded, "Stop calling my house!" He slammed the phone down on the hook and shouted at Rhonda, "Get up and fix me some dinner! You're just a lazy whore. I don't know why I stay with you and these sorry kids."

Damien said, "Dad!"

John turned to him, "Except you son. You're the only bright spot in my life. Come here boy."

Markus watched as Damien went over to their dad. John showed affection. It was one of the only times he ever did.

John said, "You make me proud son. You're the only thing your mother ever did right. Don't ever let a woman disrespect you. Put them in their place, or you'll be nothing, less than a man. You got it?"

Damien proudly said, "Yes sir, I got it."

John pointed at Markus, "You see your brother?" Damien nodded, and John continued, "He's soft. People will run over him all his life. That's why he can't get laid."

They both laughed. Rhonda looked at Markus, and he could tell she didn't want him to respond. Markus just started washing the dishes and thought about Renata. His daydreams of her took him away from the pain of the Black's home.

***

The next morning Markus stood at Renata's doorway waiting for her to come out. She came out the door, and as always he marveled at her beauty. To him her beauty wasn't just on the outside, it was inside and out. She stood for everything right, and she lived as right as she could. She always cared about people, no matter what their standing in life.

He admired her kindness and generosity. The Smith family didn't have much, but they gave whatever they had to others. Markus thought, *"One day I'm going to build an organization that will help people.*

We will provide a service to those who can't help themselves. One thing my girl has given me is the inspiration to dream big, go after big things and to have confidence in myself. Now I will reward her by getting my education and building a legacy."

She interrupted his thoughts, "Hey boo! I called you last night and mean old dad answered. He hung up on me."

Markus shook his head in disbelief. He heard the call and now he realized it was his woman that his dad hung up on. That feeling of hate resurfaced.

He looked her in the eyes, "I'm going to call that social worker today. I'm taking the first step, Renata. Will you help me?"

Renata's mouth was wide open, "Hell yes! I am there for you baby. Let's do it at lunch on the phone by the office. I have some change if you don't."

"Okay cool. Let's go before we miss the bus."

"Yeah, I'm so excited Markus. This mess is going to end!"

Markus asked, "But what if they move me away from you?"

Renata answered, "It won't matter. We can still be together. Our love will survive Markus."

Markus smiled. He knew he could love no other woman than Renata and now she was saying the same thing. He couldn't imagine himself with anyone else but Renata.

They went to the bus stop and headed to school. This wasn't going to be any other day at school. This was going to be the beginning of the end for Markus. He was going to take that step and his woman was going to be right by his side. He couldn't have dreamed it better.

***

Lunchtime came quicker than Markus ever imagined. He was waiting for Renata by the pay phone. He didn't want to make the call until she was there to support him.

In the distance, he saw her approaching. She was smiling that elegant smile. Andra joined her as she approached.

Renata happily said, "Hey boo. Andra wants to be a part of this too."

Andra smiled, "Yeah Markus I want to help also. I know I haven't said it much, but I've been praying for this day to come. Today you will see the beginning of the end of your torment, and as your friend, I want to be there too."

Before Markus could answer two more people came up behind him, "Me too Markus," shouted Paula.

Cleveland added, "You know I'm there for you bro."

Markus thought, *"Wow Renata told the whole school."*

He looked at his girl, and she said, "Well I didn't want you to think you were alone." She smiled at him, and if he was mad, he couldn't stay mad long. She was everything to him, and she only cared for him. Now he knew his friends cared for him also. For once in his life, he felt nothing but love all around him.

He said, "Well here goes." He pulled out the quarter, put it in the pay phone and dialed the number. It rang only once before she answered, "Hello, Child Protective Services, Mrs. Boykin speaking, how may I help you?"

Markus was nervous but ready, "Hi," Renata took his arm laid her head on his shoulder. He continued, "This is Markus Black, and I'm ready to talk to you now."

Mrs. Boykin responded, "That's great Markus. I can meet you at your school. Is that okay?"

"Yes, ma'am."

"Outstanding. I will be there in about an hour. I'll have the principal get you out of class so we can talk."

"Thank you, Mrs. Boykin."

She paused for a second, "No, Markus thank you. You're a brave young man for taking this first step. We will have support for you and your family. We will get you out of this situation, I promise."

"Thank you. I'll see you in a few minutes."

"I'm on my way, Markus."

Markus hung up the phone and hugged Renata. Everyone patted him on the back and shoulder. His best friends were there for him, his best friend and girlfriend was there for him. For the first time in his life, he was truly happy. His family was going to get out the abusive home life and be happy.

***

An hour went by, and Markus hadn't been called to the office. He was getting nervous by the second and the negative thoughts were creeping into his mind again. He prayed, *"Lord keep these thoughts from me. I know that I have done the right thing; I have taken the step to end this pain, for me and my family. I have saved my mother from further heartache and pain. I have saved my sister from the miserable life we have come to know as our home life. Lord, help me to be strong*

*enough to see it all, though. Let your will
be done. In Jesus name, Amen."*

Diane came into the classroom and
Markus got excited. He knew that Diane
worked in the office during this period
and she was bringing his slip to go to the
office and talk to Mrs. Boykin.

The teacher called Markus' name, and he
shot up. Diane didn't smile at him. He
didn't understand why because she was a
friend also and she had to know what was
going on. He decided to blow it off and
head to the office.

He stopped in his tracks when he got to
the office. It was not what he expected.
His dad was standing, waiting for him. He
wasn't happy.

Mr. Davis looked at Markus. Markus
thought he even had fear in his eyes. Mr.
Davis said, "Markus, your father is here to
pick you up."

Markus didn't know what to say. He
couldn't say Mrs. Boykin was on her way
because then his dad would know he
called her, so he just dropped his head
and walked out with his dad.

Markus thought God had forsaken him again. Maybe it was true what his dad said. Maybe he was worthless and would amount to nothing.

In the car, John said, "You don't think I know things do you? You think I'm just some stupid, uneducated man without a brain or connections. I'm about to show you something boy."

Markus feared for his life. He had faced his dad before and felt he was growing in his courage to face him but this time it was different. This time he felt a true coldness with his dad. It was over 90 degrees in Tampa on this day, but it was Alaska cold inside that car. Markus thought he should jump out and run but he couldn't because he not only feared for himself, he feared for his mother and sister.

Markus walked into their apartment and Rhonda, Damien and Kyanna were waiting. The entire family was home. John locked the screen door and closed the wood door. Something was about to happen, and Markus was truly afraid.

36

Renata and Andra came running down the hallway to Mrs. Boykin. Renata shouted, "What did you do? Where's Markus? Why did you tell his father?"

Mrs. Boykin tried to calm her down, "I didn't tell his father anything. I got held up by some men in suits. They rear-ended my car, and I had to stay at the accident scene. What are you guys talking about?"

Renata was crying, "Markus' dad showed up at school and took him. Mrs. Boykin, I'm afraid for him."

Andra was crying as well, "Yeah Mrs. Boykin you gotta help Markus. His dad is crazy."

"Okay, girls let me call the police now so they can meet me there." She motioned for the girls to follow her into the office.

Once in the office, Mrs. Boykin arranged to use a phone. She called the police department, "Hi this is Mrs. Veda Boykin, and I'm a social worker for the county. I believe there's a child in danger in Belmont Heights and I request a car to join me at the residence for backup."

Renata watched in fear as Mrs. Boykin listened to the police officer.

Mrs. Boykin responded, "Well no I don't."

Renata didn't get a good feeling. She couldn't hear what the officer was saying, but Mrs. Boykins' reaction was inspiring.

Mrs. Boykin shouted, "That's the craziest thing I've heard!" She then looked at the phone upset. She set the receiver down, "He hung up on me."

Renata asked, "What? Why?"

"He said if there's no imminent danger, then they can't send a car out."

Renata deeply sighed, "Oh my God...Markus."

Mr. Davis walked up to the group, "No luck with the police?"

Mrs. Boykin said, "None. I'm going over there now and see what I can do."

Renata replied, "I'm going too!"

Andra said, "Me too."

Mr. Davis responded, "I can't let you girls leave. You have more periods before schools out."

Renata looked him squarely in the eyes, "Suspend me." She walked out the door with Andra in tow.

Andra turned and said, "Me too."

Mrs. Boykin came out after them, "Come on girls."

Renata asked, "What did he say?"

Mrs. Boykin answered, "There was nothing he could say."

They hurried to the car and sped off toward Belmont Heights. Renata was truly afraid for the life of the first and only boy she loved. She was trying not to let negative thoughts into her head, but she couldn't help it.

Andra placed her hand on Renata's shoulder from the backseat. Renata was glad Andra was with her because Andra was her best friend and if Renata needed anything she knew Andra would be the one to help.

They pulled up at Markus' row of apartments, and the gunshot was louder than Renata could have imagined. In a reactionary move, her hands immediately covered her mouth. A part of her knew what happened.

37

LaJuan was playing basketball with the other kids on the court. Despite all her issues growing up, she was quite the athlete. She wanted to play on the Adams Junior High team but never got the chance.

The other kids marveled at her skills. LaJuan knocked down consecutive three-point shots to help her team win. All the kids surrounded her congratulating her but all she saw was the older cold-hearted lady standing off the court watching.

The lady motioned for LaJuan to come over to her and she obliged. It was the longest walk ever for LaJuan. Somehow she knew they found out about the phone call. She wondered what her punishment would be. She hoped it wouldn't be going to jail for life as she originally thought she should have to do.

The cold-hearted lady said, "Come with me."

LaJuan didn't respond she just followed the lady into the house and back to the office that she made the phone call from the day before.

The man was sitting there without any emotion on his face. LaJuan wondered if anyone at the house smiled.

The man stared at LaJuan hard then he asked, "Did you think that an organization that could get your charges dismissed would not find out that you came into my office without permission and made a phone call?"

LaJuan didn't know what to say. They obviously knew what she had done so should she admit it or should she deny it. If she denies it wouldn't that make it worse for her, she thought?

She decided to admit, "I just needed to let my aunt know I was okay. That's all one simple call."

The man said, "You were told to leave your past behind you. There are no phones in this house for that reason, but yet you decided you would break the rules."

LaJuan didn't say anything.

The man continued, "I have read your file, and you have taken a lot in your short life. Punishing you probably wouldn't do anything. I believe you are immune to pain. You didn't even flinch when your hand was cut to sign the contract. Therefore, I believe a proper punishment would be to remove anything that would distract you."

The man stood up, walked over to the television and turned it on, "There's an interesting news story about to come on TV. You should watch it."

LaJuan shivered with fear. Her eyes were glued to the television.

The news reporter came on, "This morning downtown traffic was halted due to an apparent suicide. Carol Johnson apparently jumped off of the 15th floor of her hotel dying on impact. She left a note stating that she couldn't live any longer knowing that she didn't help her niece, LaJuan Craig."

LaJuan was in tears. She knew her aunt didn't commit suicide. She knew these people killed her as punishment for LaJuan.

The reporter continued, "LaJuan Craig is the young lady whose murder charges were mysteriously dropped by the district attorney's office two weeks ago."

The man turned the television off and looked coldly at LaJuan, "I expect that from now on you will obey the rules because we have no more of your relatives to use as punishment. Therefore we would be forced to terminate our contract with you. I certainly hope you know what that means. Get her out of here."

The cold-hearted lady put her arm around LaJuan and led her out the room. LaJuan was agonizing in hurt and despair. She killed her mother and now her actions got the only relative who cared about her killed.

***

LaJuan was sick to her stomach when Porshia came to her and sat down. Porshia put her arm around LaJuan, "The same thing happened to me when I first got here. I thought I could buck the rules and get away with it. These people...they are not ordinary people. They see everything. The best thing to do is to do what they ask and nothing else. They will kill you. You aren't the first and trust me, you won't be the last."

LaJuan asked, "Who they kill?"

Porshia dropped her head, "I wanted some heroin so bad that I tried to do the same thing you did. I tried to call my boyfriend and they found out. They dragged him into the big man's office and shot him up with dope. He overdosed on the spot and I had to watch him die. At least they spared you that pain. The big man threatened the rest of my family. I never broke the rules again."

LaJuan said, "I guess we're stuck in this world."

"The only way out is to die. Now we all know why we signed in blood."

LaJuan said, "Thanks for comforting me Porshia. I really appreciate it."

"No problem. Didn't you live in Belmont Heights?"

LaJuan quickly looked at her, "Yeah why what's up?"

"I heard there's something big going to happen there today. You know there's a boys' school on the other side of the hill. That's where they keep our counterparts. I'm guessing someone is headed there soon."

LaJuan said, "Wow, I wonder if I know him."

38

John shouted at Markus, "You see what you did? You're bringing people into our home and breaking up this family!"

Markus shouted back, "You're breaking up this family! We don't deserve this life!"

Rhonda stood up, "Now John just calm down we'll get out of this situation."

"Calm down...what the hell you talking about?" He punched Rhonda, and she fell back, hitting her head against the television.

Markus shouted, "I'm sick of you!" He dove at his father catching him in the stomach area, and they both fell backwards.

Rhonda grabbed Kyanna, "Go upstairs, baby."

Kyanna was crying, "But, Momma!"

"Go, baby, please, go!"

Markus and his father were wrestling hard. John pulled out a gun and tried to point it at Markus, but Markus grabbed his arm and pushed it backwards.

The jerk (is this John?)caused the gun to go off and fall to the floor. John pushed Markus off of him, and Markus sat stunned. His mother was on her knees, blood was flowing from her stomach. She was trying to hold it in, but it was not working.

Markus screamed, "Momma!" He rushed to her and tried to help her hold the blood inside. She caressed his chin and smiled, "I love you, Markus." Her body went limp in Markus' arms. He shouted, "Nooooo...momma"

Kyanna screamed, "Momma, Momma!"

Markus got angry. His father was standing there emotionless while his mother was gone. He grabbed the gun and pointed it at his father.

Kyanna shouted, "Markus!"

Markus shot his father in the chest. The recoil of the gun caused Markus to fall backwards and he lost control of the gun. The gun fell to the ground, and Markus laid there stunned. His mother was dead, and he just killed his father.

Markus reached over and grabbed Kyanna. She was crying hysterically. Their world was turned upside down.

Markus saw fear consume Kyanna's face. He said, "Daddy, can't hurt us anymore Ky."

Kyanna could only utter one word, "Damien."

Markus slowly turned, and Damien was holding the gun on him and Kyanna. Markus asked, "Damien, what are you doing?"

Damien answered, "You killed my dad. For that, you're going to pay."

Markus said, "Damien don't, he killed our mother."

Damien replied, "She deserved it! If she had only done what he said, no one would be hurt. For that matter, if you hadn't called that social worker lady none of this would have happened!"

"Let Ky go Damien. She's innocent."

"No one's innocent."

Damien cocked the trigger. Markus whispered in Kyanna's ear, "When I move run out the back door."

Kyanna replied, "No..."

Markus sternly responded, "Do it. Tell Renata I will always love her."

Kyanna continued to cry. Markus quickly jumped at Damien. The gun went off the bullet hit the ceiling.

Kyanna ran as fast as she could out the front door like her brother told her to do. Damien and Markus fought over the gun until it went off.

39

Renata stood outside. She was scared. She saw Kyanna come running out of the back door of their apartment into the waiting arms of Mrs. Boykins and the police. Renata ran to her, and Kyanna immediately went to her and held her tightly.

Kyanna told Renata, "Markus said to tell you that he will always love you."

Renata put her hand over mouth and started to cry. Andra hugged Renata tightly, and they both cried. The third shot was heard, and the police decided to move in.

Kyanna said, "My brothers were fighting. Markus told me to run. I didn't want too."

Renata replied, "You did right. Markus wanted you to be safe."

Kyanna said, "My mom and dad are dead. My dad killed my mom."

Renata watched along with everyone else. The suspense was almost too much for her now. Her mom had joined them.

Finally, the police came out with Damien. His hands were cuffed behind him. Kyanna fell to the ground shouting, "No, where's Markus!"

She broke free of them. She got to Damien and hit him repeatedly before the police could grab her and pull her away.

Renata got there and grabbed Kyanna from the police. She looked at Damien, and he smirked at her and blew her a kiss.

Renata was one who wouldn't hate anyone, but she had grown to hate Damien. He was a monster, and no one could tell her otherwise.

Renata held Kyanna, and both of them cried. Mrs. Boykin came up to Renata and Renata started to cry more. She knew what she was about to say.

Mrs. Boykin said, "I'm sorry Renata. I really am."

Renata fell to her knees. She felt her mom and Andra come to her but darkness engulfed her and she fell back on the ground.

***

Renata slowly opened her eyes. She was in her apartment on the couch. Andra was right beside her smiling. Renata asked, "Was I dreaming?"

Andra's smile went away, "No boo but we'll get through this together, I promise you."

Renata held her head and started crying again. She loved Markus so much and now he was gone. Andra just held her and cried too. That's just what her best friend needed to do. At this point, no words could truly comfort Renata so Andra gave her what she needed, a best friend who would cry with her during this time.

Allison came down the stairs and took her daughter's hand. Renata asked, "What happened to Kyanna?"

Allison answered, "She's upstairs taking a bath. She's lost everyone she cared about, so I convinced Veda to let her stay with us for a while."

Renata got up. Allison asked, "Where are you going?"

Renata smiled, "To talk to my little sister."

Renata sat down by the tub and smiled at Kyanna, "Hey Ky."

Kyanna responded, "My brother loved you so I hope we can be best friends."

Renata replied, "Well…I hope we can be sisters; that's better than best friends."

Kyanna smiled, "Yeah."

Renata gave her a 'high five' and the two of them sat there and talked. Renata felt calm as she realized that she lost her boyfriend but she would take care of his sister. It was her job. She knew how much Markus loved his baby sister and Renata would love her just as much.

40

Damien never felt this way before. Something overtook his body and made him feel powerful. When he held that gun, he felt that nothing could stop him. He was angry that Markus killed his father, but he made Markus pay for it. Now he had to get out of jail. His lawyer told him he needed to plead insanity. Damien would play the game just to get out of jail.

He looked up, and the two men in suits were in his cell. To Damien, these guys were so mysterious. He remembered that he signed a contract with them so how would his situation now affect his contract? He couldn't be a big time artist and repertoire man if he was in jail.

The guard let the men into the cell and then he disappeared. The man who does all the speaking stopped in front of Damien, "Do not worry about a plea deal. You won't need a lawyer just take the deal that will be offered to you."

Damien looked at him emotionless, "You can get me out of this mess?"

"Do as I ask and we will take care of you. Remember we have a lifelong contract."

Damien cracked a smile, "I do remember."

The man turned, and they both walked out the cell. Damien laid back on the bed smirking. He knew they would get him out of the situation and he had nothing to worry about. He was going to be big in the music industry, be rich and get all the women. That's all he cared about.

***

The next day Damien received a visit from the district attorney. Damien didn't know who he was when he arrived.

The district attorney said, "Good morning Damien."

Damien replied, "Morning...who are you?"

"I'm the district attorney for Hillsborough County, and I'm here to offer you a deal."

"What deal is that?"

The district attorney smiled, "I'm sure you had visitors yesterday, so I won't bore you with details. Just sign the papers that my assistant has for you and you'll be sent to a boys' home for the next four years. After that, you'll get everything that was promised to you."

Damien sat up and took the papers from the assistant. He asked, "I can sign this, and it's legal? You know I'm only 14, right?"

"Let us worry about that Damien. By now you should see that these people rule the world. There's nothing they can't do."

Damien signed the papers and handed them to the district attorney. He signed the papers and smiled at Damien, "someone will be here to pick you up and take you to your new residence. Good luck my friend."

Damien smirked, "Who needs luck when I got the men in suits. I can do anything I want, and they'll take care of me."

The district attorney replied, "For someone so young you seem to have the system down."

Damien rubbed his chest and smiled. The district attorney left the cell and as promised someone came to pick Damien up. It was the cold-hearted lady who picked up LaJuan.

She told Damien, "Come with me. Your new life awaits."

Damien happily got up. He saw his father kill his mother by accident, his brother murdered his father, and he killed his brother. None of it seemed to bother him now. All he wanted was his fame, riches, and women.

41

They stood at the gravesite dressed in all black. Kyanna insisted that her mother and brother be buried together but separate from her father. She didn't attend his funeral, but nothing could keep her away from her mother and brother's funeral.

She was glad Damien wasn't there. The only family member she had left was the one she had grown to hate. Damien took Markus from her, and for that, she would never forgive him.

Through it all, she now had a big sister. Renata and Kyanna got along well. Kyanna even loved Allison. The state gave Allison temporary custody of Kyanna. Kyanna was praying that it would be permanent.

Renata held Kyanna's hand as the caskets were lowered into the ground. The soft soothing song being sung helped to ease the pain some for Kyanna.

After Markus had given his life to Christ, he told Kyanna everything he learned about it. Kyanna learned more from Renata. She knew she was going to give her life to Christ as well.

They got into the limo and drove back to Belmont Heights. It was painful for Kyanna to continue to live in the projects where she lost everyone she loved but the love of the Smith family overcame any pain she was feeling. Markus' other friends were helping her too.

Andra, Paula, and Diane all came back and talked to her, helping to keep her spirits up. Kyanna appreciated that so much.

Once they got home and started to change clothes, Kyanna asked Renata, "Renata do you think Markus is looking down from Heaven at us?"

Renata smiled, "I hope not right now...I'm not dressed!"

They both laughed so hard that it made their stomachs hurt. Allison came into the room and asked, "What's so funny?"

Renata answered, "I made a joke."

Allison replied, "Really?"

Renata smacked her lips, "Oh you got jokes momma." They all hugged, and Allison said, "Let's go get some ice cream!" Kyanna replied, "Yeah let's!"

The three of them left to get ice cream, and Kyanna loved her new life. She missed her mother and brother, but she was glad that she ended up in a good Christian home.

42

Four years later...

"Damien Black, you have achieved much here at the Baal Reformatory School for Boys. You have exceeded all expectations, and this body finds you ready to go out into the music world and achieve great things. You will be assigned to Fresh City Records and responsible for obtaining talent on our behalf. Do you accept this position?"

Damien stood proudly, "I do so accept and ask that my friend Don be allowed to join me."

"So granted."

For the first time in four years, Damien and Don walked off the school grounds. The Fresh City Records private jet was preparing to take them to California where they would start their new lives as A&R men.

Don said, "Yeah boy, I can't wait to get to Cali! Four years without girls...oh my God."

Damien smiled, "Dude, we ain't got to wait until Cali. I asked that we have some company on the jet...you know what I mean?"

"That's what I'm talking 'bout! Damien, you the man."

"Yeah boy, ain't nothing but the good life from now on!"

43

LaJuan walked off the campus of her school. The last four years taught her to be cold and heartless. She was repeatedly raped for three years, and the only family member who cared about her was killed just for a phone call.

She thought about the people that had it easy and still complained. They didn't know what a tough life was, but LaJuan did. She was taught to be a cold, heartless killer...emotionless like the men in suits. She was taught to be deceiving and trust no one.

She was rated highest in her class. No one did it better than LaJuan. She was physically fit and could fire a weapon better than any man.

Her first job was simple. She had to make the death of a famous singer who had turned on the group look like a suicide. She thought, *"It will be easy, she's on drugs anyway. I'll just pump some in her system and gently hold her head under the water. No one will know the difference."*

LaJuan got on a plane and headed to California to begin her new life as an assassin for the men in suits.

44

Renata was a senior at State University. She dedicated her life to the ending domestic violence and created the Markus G. Black Foundation. Her foundation was building to help battered women and abused children.

Kyanna was a junior in high school, and she spent every chance helping Renata with the foundation. Renata and Kyanna put together the first annual Belmont Heights Family Day and Renata was hard at work.

It was a typical hot Saturday afternoon when Penny Davis approached Renata. Renata said, "Hi Penny. You guys ready to blow this place up?"

Penny replied, "We are. Thanks for giving us this opportunity."

Renata responded, "Oh it's not a problem. Markus was your age when...well you know so seeing you grow up to a beautiful young lady just inspired me to have you guys sing. How old are your sisters?"

"Nya is 14 and Raine is ten. We've been singing for as long as I can remember. I don't remember Markus, but I heard good things about him. I know you miss him."

"I do, but his death has inspired this foundation and saved a lot of lives. Thanks to Markus at least seven other kids have come out of abusive homes here in Belmont Heights. One of them is Markus' sister Kyanna. Look at her she's enjoying life now."

Penny smiled, "Yeah Ky is cool. She's in my marketing class at Tech."

Renata said, "Great, well I have a ton of stuff to do so I'll chat with you later okay."

"Okay...thanks again!"

Renata smiled, "You welcome." She watched as Penny walked off toward her sisters. She remembers when she was 16 and in love with Markus. The last four years she hadn't been able to date anyone else. She knew inside that Markus would have wanted her to go on with her life but she just couldn't. Now just wasn't the time. She had too much work to do in the community.

Renata saw some men standing near the Davis girls. They caught her attention because it was near a hundred degrees and they were wearing suits. She watched them as they watched the girls. When Renata went to ask security about the men they walked away.

Allison approached Renata, "Hey baby, you got everything under control?"

"Yes, ma'am. There were some strange men watching the Davis girls. I went to ask the guard to check them out but then they walked to that limo and drove off. Do you think I should report it?"

Allison rolled her eyes at her daughter, "If it's one thing we've learned from all of this is that we need to report what we learn and not keep secrets. Yes, baby, we need to report it. Those girl's lives could be at stake."

Renata watched Raine Davis as she danced and sung to her friends. She had talent, and no one could argue that. Renata knew she would be a big star if she kept singing.

Epilogue

Twelve years later…

The years were kind to LaJuan. She still commanded respect and admiration of every man she came into contact with. She walked into the headquarters of the building where she worked. They called her in because she had a new assignment. As bad as her life started she now enjoyed anything she wanted when she wanted. When her assignments came up, she handled her business.

She stepped into the all too familiar conference room and stood squarely in the middle of the room, facing the man she had come to recognize and respect as the leader.

He said, "On time as always I see."

LaJuan responded, "Punctuality is necessary for my business."

He nodded, "We have a new assignment for you. Damien Black is going to sign a new singer. Her name is Lorraine "Raine" Davis. We need you to go to Fresh City

339

Records, befriend Raine and keep an eye on her and Damien."

LaJuan deeply sighed. The leader continued, "You are not happy with this assignment?"

"Baby sitting...really? You know my feelings on Damien Black; I'd just as soon kill him."

The leader said, "Raine is the best talent in years. We do not want Damien to destroy this opportunity for us. Yes, we need for you to be her friend. Stay close to her and let us know what happens. If necessary, you will have your opportunity to terminate Mr. Black's contract. Understood?"

"Yes, I understand. Go to California and babysit with the hope of taking out Damien."

"See to it." The man rose from his luxurious seat and walked out of the room as emotionless as he has always been.

LaJuan nodded her head and whispered under her breath, *"I so hope I get the chance to kill you, Damien!"*

www.ingramcontent.com/pod-product-compliance
Lightning Source LLC
LaVergne TN
LVHW051451080426
835509LV00017B/1733